Endorsemen

TRANSFORMING PARISH COMMUNICATIONS

"As someone who started his career in *old* media, and reluctantly got into new media, I'm thrilled Scot is encouraging Catholics to engage in new media. It's not a question of 'if' Catholics should be involved in new media ... but a question of 'how'. Scot answers that question of 'how' perfectly. And he, just maybe, makes the rest of us feel guilty we're not doing more! Well, guilt is good in this case. New media is the New Evangelization." — **Lino Rulli, host of *The Catholic Guy* on SiriusXM's The Catholic Channel (three-time Emmy winner)**

"I have always believed that the struggle is not between new and old evangelization but good and bad evangelization. Good evangelization relies on good communications and a Catholic understanding of broadcasting, social media, and how we reach people in the 21st century. This book is an outstanding guide to that process and is essential reading if we are to move forward as Catholics in the modern age." — **Michael Coren, author and broadcaster**

"For years, whenever Catholics asked me for new media advice, I'd simply say: 'Look to Boston'. The Archdiocese of Boston has long been a shining light in the digital world, and Scot Landry is much to thank. He remains a pioneering leader in Catholic new media, which is why I'm so thankful for his new book. It's rare you get to learn directly from someone at the top of his field. But this book delivers practical, straightforward tips on how to harness the most powerful technologies our Church has ever known. Read it, apply it, and join millions of Catholics in giving the Internet a Christian soul." — **Brandon Vogt, author of *The Church and New Media* and content director at Word on Fire**

"Scot Landry is to be complimented on this most timely and useful publication. He both reminds us why the Church needs to be present in the 'new continent' of social media and tells us how to make our presence effective. He shows us how the traditional welcome offered by our parishes to those who come searching for a 'home,' where they may find mercy and healing, hope and meaning, can be extended to far more people if we are attentive to participating in the conversations and dialogue that are emerging across new media platforms.

"Scot's great achievement is in offering very concrete suggestions as to how individual Catholics and parish communities can take their first steps into the digital space. His suggestions are eminently practical and serve to remove some of the fear factors that may inhibit parish initiatives. He puts us on our way and encourages us to be 'thoughtful practitioners' who learn from doing. As we become more at home as 'citizens' of the networks, we will be better able to evaluate how effective we are in listening to, conversing with, encouraging, and, ultimately, bringing to meet Christ those we encounter in this environment. If we share our learning with one another in the Church, we can grow together and share the Good News of God's love with all those men and women for whom social media are an essential dimension of their lives.

"Scot has very generously shared with us his accumulated learning and experience in working with new media in the mission of the Church. His enthusiasm and competence make him a great guide and companion for those who are venturing into this arena; his great familiarity with the area and the thoroughness of his presentation ensure he has much to offer to those who are already engaged." — **Monsignor Paul Tighe, secretary of the Pontifical Council for Social Communications**

"The idea of the New Evangelization is so often put forth in such abstract terms that many Catholics who want to be involved in it are at a loss as to how to do so. There are plenty of books that cover the 'why' of the New Evangelization, and dreadfully few books that cover the 'how.' Landry starts, not by showing us how to save the world (an indomitable task that can cause us to feel like abandoning evangelization efforts altogether), but rather how to embrace the means of salvation offered to us, and extend the joy of our own faith lives to the community we meet with every Sunday — the Catholic brothers and sisters in our own parishes who we're embarrassed to admit that we don't really know." — **Matt Swaim, host of *Son Rise Morning Show*, EWTN Radio**

"In his 2014 World Communications Day message, Pope Francis called the Internet 'a gift from God' through which 'the Christian message can reach "to the ends of the earth." ' If that's our mandate in the digital age, then Scot Landry's *Transforming Parish Communications: Growing the Church Through New Media* is your instruction manual." — **Kevin Knight, NewAdvent.org**

"Men and women today increasingly find themselves lost online in a world of false encounter. They're often feeling alone, unsatisfied, unhappy, and certainly removed from the life of the Church. Catholics must be present there, inviting them in. Scot Landry walks parishes through opening church doors online in welcoming ways, to invite our brothers and sisters to encounter Christ and consider the sacramental life in community." — **Kathryn Jean Lopez, editor-at-large at National Review Online and nationally syndicated columnist**

"As Pope Francis said in his first World Communications Day statement, 'The Internet … offers immense possibilities for encounter and solidarity … [and] is something truly good, a gift from God.' *Transforming Parish Communications* is just what the doctor ordered. It will help parishes apply this gift of the Internet, in particular new media, through practical yet purposeful ways. This book is a tool, with the potential to transform parish life and have an even broader impact on the New Evangelization." — **Teresa Tomeo, author, syndicated Catholic talk-show host, and motivational speaker**

"Throughout its history, the Church has engaged challenges arising from various cultural developments and declines. With God's graces and the gifts of the Holy Spirit, individuals and communities have found the insights that allow the Church to transpose its presence in the world so as to fulfill the mission of Christ, the Incarnate Word. We all know the enormous technical developments that have changed the means and systems of communication; we are the ones who must help to effect the contemporary transposition so as to bring the Lord and the Gospel to those in our world and culture. It is notable that Scot Landry's book, *Transforming Parish Communications: Growing the Church Through the New Media*, provides many sophisticated and practical insights as we face the challenges in evangelizing in our time." — **Most Reverend Arthur L. Kennedy, Ph.D., auxiliary bishop, Archdiocese of Boston, and episcopal vicar for the New Evangelization**

"Toss out all your parish's excuses for not using new media to mobilize evangelizers to bring people back to the Catholic Church. Scot Landry has expertly covered every angle, from creating content and launching it online to engaging others and making parishes the exciting hubs of evangelization God means for them to be. The appendices alone are worth the price of the book." — **Greg Willits, author of *The New Evangelization and You*, co-host of *The Catholics Next Door*, and co-founder of NewEvangelizers.com**

"The next generation of parishioners is growing up online. They tweet and text from their smartphones while reading books and watching videos on their iPads and eReaders. For the Church to reach this generation, we need to all be on the digital continent that is the Internet. *Transforming Parish Communications* provides a practical road map for every church to communicate and evangelize using this new technology that now permeates today's modern life." — **Joe Luedtke, president of Liturgical Publications, Inc., and editor of CatholicTechTalk.com**

"A beautifully woven guide that is profoundly relevant and pedagogically sound for the new digital age. It skillfully outlines authentic best practices of new media with our universal call to the New Evangelization. As a practitioner in digital strategy at Harvard and a practicing Catholic, it's exciting to see this type of book written. I'm heartened that Scot found a way to effortlessly dovetail the complexities of religion and technology in the pages of this impressive read." — **Matt Weber, digital strategist and producer at Harvard University and author of *Fearing the Stigmata***

"*Transforming Parish Communications* by Scot Landry is a must read for pastors and parish teams. Landry asks *the* question for pastors: Why use scant resources to become a digital immigrant, and train staff and parishioners to do the same? The answer comes from the heart of Church teaching: the Internet requires 'a soul,' and 'digital natives' need to be evangelized by 'digital missionaries.' The book provides all the tools needed for parishes to enter the digital continent, including step-by-step instructions for creating a 'new media commission,' mentoring volunteers, and messaging. Envisioning what can happen if the practicing 17-plus percent effectively leveraged social media to invite back the missing 80-plus percent, it foresees the possibility of a single parish evangelizing literally millions of Catholics!" — **Janet Benestad, cabinet secretary for New Evangelization, Archdiocese of Boston**

"Knowing, loving, and proclaiming Jesus Christ is both a personal and digital opportunity and responsibility. Scot Landry has become an expert in the new media, and this book is a powerful, pastoral 'why to' *and* 'how to' evangelize through new social communications. Our people are technologically savvy; let's meet them where they are! As one who provides leadership training and consulting, I recommend *Transforming Parish Communications: Growing the Church Through New Media* because it equips parish and diocesan leadership with an organized and accessible means to reach all — and particularly those who are lost or distant from us and Him. This rich resource enables a team or commission to actually prioritize and plan 'evangelizing' with greater care and confidence." — **Father Bill Dickinson, D.Min., vice-president of episcopal and client services, Catholic Leadership Institute**

"I believe that this book is a significant tool for parishes as they start to embrace the task of the New Evangelization. Pastors and their teams will find this tool to be of inestimable use as they develop strategies for engaging the new media in that task." — **Father Paul Soper, director of pastoral planning, Archdiocese of Boston**

"*Transforming Parish Communications: Growing the Church Through New Media* makes a critical and needed contribution to the emerging dialogue about new media and its impact on bringing Catholics and non-Catholics closer to a personal relationship with God. This well-reasoned book is a clarion call for deeper levels of engagement that are possible through a new and broad array of technologies and approaches that enliven and enrich our faith." — **John Corcoran, CEO of Trinity Partners, LLC, president of Legatus of Boston, and trustee at iCatholic Media, Inc.**

"Good Catholic parishes reach parishioners and potential newcomers on Sundays. Great Catholic parishes reach them 24/7 with digital media. Move your parish from good to great with Scot Landry's *Transforming Parish Communications*. Landry's expertise champions clear communications strategies — a how-to for building relationships and delivering faith-based messages in person, online, and direct to parishioners' smartphones. Joining the Church's New Evangelization vision with local parish practicality, this easy-to-read volume offers resources and a plan to grow your parish mission." — **Pat Gohn, author of** *Blessed, Beautiful, and Bodacious* **and host of the** *Among Women* **podcast**

"Scot Landry's book offers a great opportunity to parishes. You would be capable of creating and implementing a social media plan for your parish or Church group once you have studied this book. It provides a full plan, complete with everything you need to succeed. What a great resource!" — **Andreas Widmer, director of entrepreneurship programs at The Catholic University of America and author of** *The Pope & the CEO*

"Scot Landry's great gift is his ability to both see the forest *and* the trees. His passion for spreading the Word and his amazing experiences as a technology business leader, in the media and working for the Church, make him uniquely suited to guide the next wave of Church leaders towards optimizing this 'New Media' Evangelization." — **Bob Allard, CEO of Extension Engine (web and mobile solutions provider)**

"As a theologian, I am frequently asked what the New Evangelization means concretely for priests and laypeople. Now I can point people to this book. In it, Scot Landry gives us deep insight into human functioning, seasoned with his keen organizational skills. The result is a practical, easy-to-work program of action for parishes and individuals who know they need to evangelize better but just don't know how to start. This book shows you how to harness the power of new media in order to reach the majority of baptized Catholics who are missing from parishes, as well as how to make inroads into the secular marketplace of ideas. If we really believed that the Gospel of Jesus Christ brings the deepest fulfillment to every human being, we couldn't help but evangelize. Scot Landry shows us how to do it in 140 characters." — **Angela Franks, Ph.D., author of *Contraception and Catholicism***

"*Growing the Church Through New Media* introduces 'digital missionary' to our faith-sharing vocabulary. Scot Landry meticulously presents parishes a plan of action that will empower parishioners — many of whom may not ordinarily consider doing so — with innovative ways to courageously share their Catholic faith. With concrete strategies and advice to overcome fear and obstacles, this book will help each of us reach beyond our church walls like never before." — **Allison Gingras, founder of Reconciled To You and a Catholic new media consultant**

"I believe that Scot Landry has pinpointed an important aspect of evangelization in the 'digital continent,' the parish, which I believe is the next big thing in 'new' media. We cannot continue to rely on diocesan efforts alone; the parish can and must be the center of the New Evangelization for the 'digital continent' and beyond. I believe everyone involved in parish ministry needs to read this book." — **Father Chip Hines, pastor of three parishes and host of CatholicTV's *Spotlight* show**

"The power of Catholic radio and Catholic new media allows our Catholic community to reach those away from the Church and to strengthen all of us in the practice of our great faith. Scot Landry has learned a great amount about sharing the faith effectively through new technologies. In this book, he provides both a wealth of inspiration for the New Evangelization as well as practical implementation ideas for parishes everywhere." — **Chris Kelley, station manager at 1060AM WQOM, Catholic radio, in Boston**

Growing
the Church
Through
New Media

TRANSFORMING
PARISH
COMMUNICATIONS

SCOT LANDRY

FOREWORD BY CARDINAL SEÁN O'MALLEY, O.F.M. CAP.

Our Sunday Visitor Publishing Division
Our Sunday Visitor, Inc.
Huntington, Indiana 46750

To my wife, Ximena, for your constant love and support through the journey of living "The Good Catholic Life" in our home, church, and community. I love you.

TABLE OF CONTENTS

FOREWORD

In April 2013, as part of our Archdiocese of Boston's celebration of the Year of Faith, I traveled with 29 priests to the Holy Land.[1] One of the most moving experiences was visiting the Upper Room. We all reflected on how the disciples hid there in fear and confusion, lacking a sense of outward mission and purpose. Christ then sent them the Holy Spirit, and the disciples were transformed. Courage replaced fear (11 of the 12 apostles would ultimately be martyred), understanding replaced confusion, and they gained a deep sense of purpose. They realized their experience of Jesus' sacrificial death and resurrection was truly Good News, and it needed to be shared. Their focus turned outward toward all those they were called to evangelize. They never returned to the Upper Room again!

There are over one billion Catholics in the world today, and we are indebted to those first disciples, and all those who followed them, for handing on the faith to each subsequent generation, sometimes in very challenging circumstances and often at the cost of their own lives. We are entrusted today with that same mission.

We are conscious of the fact that so many Catholics here in the Archdiocese of Boston, across the United States, and across the world do not join us regularly for the celebration of the Sunday Eucharist or participate in the life of our community. This reality saddens all of us in the Church and provides the motivation for the New Evangelization. A good indicator of whether we are evangelized is whether we, in turn, are evangelizers. An important part of *living* the Catholic faith is *sharing* the Catholic faith. The success of the New Evangelization can be measured by how many Catholics are emboldened to become evangelizers.

As our society becomes increasingly secular, it takes greater courage to share our faith and our selves with others. We risk rejection every time we walk across the room to greet someone, every time we share the Church's teachings in love, and every time we invite someone to join us for the Sunday Eucharist. Like those first disciples, we, too, need to request the gifts of the Holy Spirit to help us in the fundamental task of evangelization that we have as Christ's followers and as a Church.

The various tools of new media provide a great opportunity for us to accompany others in their journey in this life and to witness to Christ's transformative grace in our lives. New media allows us to make an impact on people next door and halfway across the world — at the same time! Relationships can be formed and nurtured on the digital continent and allow for conversations that lead to the sharing of prayers, links to great faith-related articles and videos, and invitations to Mass or other parish gatherings.

I have seen personally the transformative power of new media. When my staff and I discussed the possibility of launching a blog in September 2006 (CardinalSeansBlog.org), I was hesitant. None of us knew where it would lead. From the first post, it attracted readers from all across the archdiocese and throughout the world. It has grown into a weekly opportunity for me to share experiences that I think can encourage others in living our beautiful Catholic faith. It has been a joy to travel to so many places and hear from so many that read my blog weekly, especially from those who say they like to share it with others.

In November 2012, we faced a very damaging ballot initiative in Massachusetts, which aimed to legalize assisted suicide. With fewer than two months before the election, polls showed that Massachusetts' voters were in favor of the initiative by 49 points (68 percent to 19 percent).[2] Through an effective advertising campaign, the use of Twitter, prayer, and the effective mobilization of communities of faith-based groups, pro-life groups, disability-rights groups, and many medical professionals, we were able to defeat this assisted suicide initiative (51 percent to 49 percent). Social media allowed us, on a limited budget, to share important articles, videos, news stories, and much more through my blog and Twitter account (@CardinalSean).

We are called to do many things in the Church, but the primary mandate given by Jesus and powered by the Holy Spirit is to evangelize. The Church exists to evangelize, to share the Good News with all people. Correspondingly, every Catholic is asked to make it his or her own responsibility to reach out and encourage others to join with us in Christ's family, the Church. Our preaching, both in word and deed, is the way we evangelize. We can transform the culture around us by living our faith well and embracing the spiritual and corporal works of mercy. We have the mission "to repair the world," what the Jews call *Tikkun olam*.

Over time, the word "evangelization" has developed negative connotations for some and has been misunderstood to be an aggressive or manipulative form of proselytism. Catholic evangelization is never proselytism. Evangelization always seeks to propose our faith and never to impose it. It is always respectful of human dignity and authentic freedom.

There are three ways to evangelize. We *witness*, which is the simple living of our faith through our good actions and virtuous deeds. We *share* our faith in an explicit way, typically by describing how God is working in our lives. We *invite* others to experience Christ's saving love by walking with us in our Catholic Church.

If the Church exists to evangelize, the parish is the chief venue where that activity must take place. Our parishes must be true centers of evangelization. The parish is the place where most Catholics regularly experience the Church. Evangelization inevitably involves the parish community because, ultimately, we aim to invite people to the Eucharist, to the table of the Lord. An evangelizing spirit must touch every dimension of Catholic parish life.

Our task in our parishes is to foster ongoing conversion, turning consumers into disciples and disciple-makers. Social media — such as Twitter, Facebook, blogs, and other tools — provide a great opportunity for each of us to witness, share, and invite.

In the Archdiocese of Boston, we have put many forms of Catholic media at the service of the New Evangelization. In 2010, we formed the Secretariat for Catholic Media, and I appointed Scot

Landry our first cabinet secretary. We have sought to utilize our ministries of the CatholicTV Network, *The Pilot* newspaper, Pilot Bulletins, Pilot Printing, Pilot New Media, our radio apostolate, and *The Good Catholic Life* radio program to further all of our significant archdiocesan initiatives, particularly to reach out to those outside the Church with an invitation to come home and then to help all of us grow as disciples. These tools will be very important as we try to structure our parishes, and the entire Archdiocese of Boston, for the work of the New Evangelization.

In this book, Scot Landry explains why it is critical for parishes, as hubs of the New Evangelization, to embrace new media. He indicates what the essential new media tools are for parishes today, shares practical strategies for how to implement them, and describes how these tools can transform parish communications. I am confident that Scot's practical wisdom, passion for evangelization, and enthusiasm for new media will help parish leaders overcome any hesitancy about embracing these new methods. We would like all parishes to have a program for engaging those on the digital continent and leading them to be transformed by the grace of the sacraments and the love of the Christian community within the Church.

Thank you for everything you are doing, and everything you will do, to bring Christ's light and love to all those in this new frontier of new media.

God bless you.

✠ CARDINAL SEÁN O'MALLEY, O.F.M. CAP.

Archbishop of Boston

INTRODUCTION

The papal conclave in March 2013 is when the world first met Pope Francis. It is also when I truly appreciated the power of new media to share our faith with those far from the Church.

COVERING THE CONCLAVE

Cardinal Seán O'Malley, archbishop of Boston, had encouraged me as his cabinet secretary for Catholic Media to see the conclave as an opportunity for evangelization. So I went to Rome with my colleague George Martell to provide a "Boston Catholic pilgrim's experience" of being in Rome during this historic transition from Pope Benedict XVI to a new pope. We planned to record the archdiocese's daily radio show, *The Good Catholic Life*, to blog each day, to share George's photos and videos, and to invite prayer requests that we would take to pray at the tomb of the first pope, St. Peter.

We arrived in Rome on March 4. Then things got very interesting for all of us from Boston, as the Italian newspapers and other journalists started mentioning Cardinal Seán as a *papabile* (papal contender). Everywhere I went, hotel workers, cab drivers, Italian citizens, and tourists were mentioning that the Capuchin Franciscan cardinal from Boston was their hope to become pope. Two months earlier the idea that we could have an American pope in our lifetime seemed far-fetched. Now both Cardinal Seán and Cardinal Dolan from New York were receiving a lot of attention and buzz.

My daily blog posts from Rome on TheGoodCatholicLife.com started to receive worldwide hits because of our detailed descriptions of Cardinal Seán's activities and the audio recordings of the American cardinals' popular press conferences from the Pontifical North American College. Renowned blogs and Catholic websites like Whispers in the Loggia and New Advent started linking to these posts, remarking that "no one in the [English-speaking] world right now is covering the conclave like you are, as pilgrims, not as journalists."[3]

Friends, whom I had not been in contact with since high school and college, were now reading these posts or listening to the daily radio show. Many parents in our local school community were telling my wife how much they enjoyed my coverage. Often these conversations began something like, "I was raised Catholic" or "I don't go to Church any longer," and then concluded by saying that despite being away from the Church they were excited followers, particularly because of the local angle and witness of someone they knew who was privileged to be in Rome.

On the afternoon of March 13, we stood in the pouring rain in St. Peter's Square expecting black smoke. We had left a lot of our expensive media equipment in the hotel because of the rain and because it was still early in the conclave. When the crowd reacted to the white smoke emanating from the chimney on the top of the Sistine Chapel, and then the announcement that our new Holy Father would be Cardinal Jorge Maria Bergoglio, from Argentina, who would be taking the name Francis, we were able to capture it all on our iPhones, Zoom recorders and George's camera. Along with the crowd, we were moved by Pope Francis' profound and humble gesture of asking for our prayers for him. On our blog that evening, we were able to recount, "What it was like to be in St. Peter's Square when Pope Francis was elected" and then to share with the world the up-close experiences of a Catholic pilgrim from Boston.[4] People still wrote to me months later to tell me that they had found that post through a Google search and greatly appreciated the firsthand account of the reaction from Rome.

When we post something in new media, we never know whom or where it will reach.

EMBRACING NEW MEDIA AT A DIOCESAN AND PARISH LEVEL

Seven years earlier in 2006, Cardinal Seán invited me to join his cabinet as the secretary for Institutional Advancement. I had known and admired him since 1992, when my twin brother, Roger, became a seminarian for the Diocese of Fall River, Massachusetts, which Bishop O'Malley had been leading at the time. When Bishop O'Malley was named archbishop of Boston in 2003, in the middle of the biggest crisis this archdiocese ever had, I knew he was the right person to guide us through the challenges, to comfort all those wounded by the Church, and to eventually lead a renewal. As someone who loves the Church, I was honored to have the opportunity to assist Cardinal Seán in these efforts as a member of his team.

The work of institutional advancement (known also as development or fund-raising) is closely connected with the ministry of communications. We wanted parishioners in the Archdiocese of Boston to see the progress we were making and to once again appreciate the beauty of the Church. My passion for telling the heartwarming stories of people living our Catholic faith each day through both Catholic media and non-Catholic media made an impression on Cardinal Seán and some of the other members of his cabinet, and soon I was asked to oversee the archdiocese's Catholic media ministries in addition to the development organization.

We are blessed in the Archdiocese of Boston to have one of the largest and best Catholic television networks in the world, CatholicTV, and America's oldest Catholic newspaper, *The Pilot*. Cardinal Seán recognized that those ministries were doing a great job of sharing news and formational content with their audiences, but that they were not reaching everyone we as a Church hoped to reach. I was part of a small team that helped Cardinal Seán launch his blog, CardinalSeansBlog.org, and then a weekly email from him that aggregated links to his blog other content from ministries across the archdiocese so that we could reach additional people.

The more time I spent working with Catholic media, the more convinced I became that we needed to do more in the area of new media and social media at both the diocesan and parish levels. Dom Bettinelli and George Martell, colleagues in the archdiocese's Institutional Advancement office, were equally passionate about this goal, and we all started taking on various aspects of new and social media for the archdiocese in addition to our other duties. Despite having perhaps the most new-media-friendly cardinal in the world as our archbishop, the budget challenges facing the Archdiocese of Boston presented many obstacles that we needed to overcome in our advocacy for greater priority and staffing resources for the creation of a new media office.

In July 2010, Cardinal Seán formally inaugurated the Catholic Media Secretariat and named me the first cabinet secretary. While I missed working in the development function, I was happy that Cardinal Seán was affording Dom, George, and I the opportunity to focus on growing the archdiocese's capabilities in new media at the diocesan and parish levels and to work toward Cardinal Seán's goals to add Catholic radio, bulletin, and printing ministries to our media capabilities.

At the diocesan level, we soon heard from new media pioneers throughout the United States. We concluded that we were the first diocese that had a true office for new media (i.e., more than one person). It became clear that many of these new media leaders were counting on us to have success in Boston so that they could present our results to their own bishops. They hoped that strong results in Boston might convince their bishops and diocesan CFOs of the need to expand new media outreach in their dioceses. We also experienced a huge demand from colleagues in the Archdiocese of Boston ministries to leverage new media tools to communicate information with their audiences and to dialogue with them.

At the parish level, we conducted an audit of every parish's website and social media presence. We discovered that roughly a third of our parishes had an okay-to-good website, a third had an outdated website, and a third had no website at all. Only a handful of parishes had any social media presence.

We began a process to help parishes in the Archdiocese of Boston to grow their capabilities in digital media. The insights and fruits of that process over the past four years are the foundation of this book.

To be candid, we still have far fewer than the goal of having 100 percent of our parishes with an up-to-date website and with a strong social media presence. Progress is being made, however, and our efforts here in Boston continue. Pastors and parish staff members have been honest about their questions on these new media platforms and the financial and human challenges they face in implementing the types of ideas outlined in this book. We have learned from their feedback, and I hope readers of this book will too.

About Me — a Digital Immigrant

Pope Benedict XVI, in his 2009 message for World Communications Day, shared the idea of the "digital continent." Like missions to physical continents, there are digital "natives" and "immigrants" (newcomers).

I think of "digital natives" as early adopters of new platforms who like to be on the cutting edge, and those to whom technology comes easily. I am much more a "digital immigrant" from a technical perspective. I appreciate technology and strive to learn it, but it does not come as easily to me as it did to my new media colleagues Dom and George at the Archdiocese of Boston, those I met at various new media conferences over the past few years, and certainly everyone who contributed chapters along with me in Brandon Vogt's great book *The Church and New Media*.[5]

When I was approached to write this book, my initial reaction was to think that it might be better if it were written by a Catholic digital "native." After further reflection, however, I thought that since the vast majority of Catholics are digital immigrants like me, then a fellow "immigrant" might be better positioned to encourage parishes to embrace new forms of media to grow the Church, just as I tried to do in my role at the Archdiocese of Boston.

Like many of you reading this book, I often struggle with technology and have taken a while to embrace all the new media platforms. I hope this book will speak to fellow digital immigrants and help them conclude that new media can be very helpful to the Church, to our parishes, and to each of us who choose to embrace these tools.

For me, new media outreach is much more about communication than technology. As a Church, new media allow us to share the Good News, connect with friends (old and new), listen to them, dialogue with them, and accompany one another through our journey in this life. As I will share later in the book, social media also involve a change in the culture of our communications, which I believe presents great opportunities for parish communities if we learn about these shifts and bring the wisdom and love of the Church to these new places of encounter.

New media platforms can be among the Church's most powerful tools of outreach and evangelization.

ABOUT THIS BOOK

My goal for this book is that everyone who reads it at the parish level will grow in the passion to adopt new media as a central tool of outreach and evangelization.

I write, first, to pastors, hoping that they will champion this effort, and then to parish staff members who can help ensure that new media outreach is coordinated with everything else that happens in the parish. My ultimate target audience, however, is those whom I hope pastors appoint to a soon-to-be-created New Media Outreach Commission (NMOC) and those who will support the NMOC's work. This book, I hope, will make your important work easier: to transform parish communications by adopting new media tools.[6]

This book is structured around three central questions:

1. Why must the Church be present in new media to fulfill its mission? Related to this is the question: What are the main reasons parishes have not fully embraced new media yet?

2. How can the Church best implement new media evangelization without over-burdening very busy parish priests and parish staff members?

3. What are the essential things parishes need to know to begin utilizing digital media effectively?

We will start in the first two chapters with the Church's mission to reach those "lost" from the Church and then discuss recent messages and actions regarding new media from our popes and social media leaders in the Vatican. We will also explore some of the reasons why some parishes have been hesitant to embrace new media, examine what can be done to overcome this resistance, and present a vision for parishes to be "animating hubs" of new media evangelization.

Then we will focus on a specific strategy to implement this vision at a parish level through the formation of a New Media Outreach Initiative led by a New Media Outreach Commission (NMOC). Example NMOC charters and timelines are included in the chapters and also in the appendices to make it easier to form a NMOC and then to begin its work of growing the Church through new media.

Next we will discuss practical new media topics, such as creating a consistent digital identity, establishing a strong website and blog, sharing content and engaging in dialogue through social media, and then financing all this work though an online-giving platform linked to the parish website.

The appendices and the companion website, ParishGuideTo NewMedia.com, are essential components of this book project because they include detailed implementation resources, visual demonstrations, and a glossary of new media terms. The appendices contain many items, such as timelines and messages to aid a parish's NMOC in its work. The website allows me to update links as new media evolves and to show visuals of various media tools that do not always work well in a printed-book format. This approach, I hope, will also lengthen the book's usefulness to you and your parish.

Thanks for sharing this journey. Let us begin by reviewing Christ's passion to reach the lost.

SUMMARY POINTS

- The author is a "digital immigrant" writing primarily to other "digital immigrants," who help lead the more than 17,000 parishes in the United States, as well as to parishioners who hope their parishes will become true hubs of the New Evangelization.

- Cardinal O'Malley's experience blogging from Rome during the 2013 conclave was transformative and gave him direct experience of the power and promise of new media for the work of the New Evangelization.

- Pastors and parish leaders are very busy. This book is about why the Church must be present in new media to fulfill its mission, how can the Church best implement new media evangelization without over-burdening very busy parish priests and parish staff members, and about the essential things parishes need to know to begin utilizing digital media effectively.

REFLECTION AND DISCUSSION QUESTIONS

Do you come to the experience of reading this book as a digital native, digital immigrant, or somewhere in between?

•••

How have you been encouraged through tools of new media to grow in your Catholic faith?

•••

What do you hope to learn about new media as you read this book?

Chapter One

REACHING THE LOST

"Are we still a Church capable of warming hearts? A Church capable of leading people back to Jerusalem? Of bringing them home? Jerusalem is where our roots are: Scripture, catechesis, sacraments, community, friendship with the Lord, Mary and the apostles.... Are we still able to speak of these roots in a way that will revive a sense of wonder at their beauty?"[7]

POPE FRANCIS, MEETING WITH THE
BISHOPS OF BRAZIL, JULY 28, 2013

Pope Francis has been asking the Church and the world provocative questions since his election on March 13, 2013.

Few questions have been as jarring as the one above, delivered to bishops during his apostolic visit to World Youth Day in Brazil. As the leader of one billion Catholics throughout the world, his rhetorical query of whether the Church could still move people with the Gospel message made for media headlines across the world.

In the months since, I have heard and seen this question repeated often. It is clear that the Church is capable of warming hearts today by introducing people to Jesus and encouraging them to begin a deeper and everlasting friendship with Christ. In that way, we can help their hearts to burn just like the disciples whom Jesus met on the road to Emmaus on Resurrection Day (Lk 24:13-35).

Pope Francis' question, however, was not meant to be theoretical. Like so much of his pastoral approach, the pope is asking: *In our day-to-day priorities and approaches, is the Church acting in a way that will encourage an encounter with the Son of God so that lives will be transformed?*

A WORLDWIDE EXAMINATION OF CONSCIENCE

At all levels of the Church — the Vatican, dioceses, parishes, families, and individuals — Pope Francis is inspiring an examination of conscience.

How hard are we striving to connect people — close friends, occasional acquaintances, and those on the margins — with the person of Jesus Christ? How much effort are we expending at each of these levels to share Christ's saving message with others, which is the task of evangelization? Do we see this as an important part of the way we follow Christ individually and collectively in our parishes, or do we behave as if it's some other person's or group's responsibility?

If we do have the passion for this outreach, the next question concerns means. Are we actually using an approach that will reach people today and allow them to encounter Christ so that he can warm their hearts? Or are we using older approaches or only those within our comfort zones? Are our approaches effective? How are we even measuring the effectiveness of our approaches?

When we think of evangelization campaigns, most of us envision neighborhood door-to-door outreach efforts and personal one-on-one faith sharing. These types of campaigns work because they are proactive efforts to go where people are, greet them in a friendly manner, ask if there are things that the parish can pray for, share information on parish liturgies and ministries, and invite them to participate in parish life. These are positive encounters. They require an energetic group of organizers and many parishioners to participate in the outreach. Few parishes in my part of the country, the northeastern United States, run these campaigns today. A large reason is because personal, on-the-spot, one-on-one evangelization is not considered a comfortable activity for many Catholics for a variety of reasons. It is often not the best entry-level outreach idea if we want there to be large participation.

Today there is a more effective broad-based, entry-level evangelization approach.

OUTREACH ON THE DIGITAL CONTINENT

In the year 2014 and beyond, social media allows us to reach people where they are gathering for information sharing and conversation. It offers the potential to attract a far higher participation rate of parishioners than standard evangelization campaigns because vast multitudes are already present there; we just need to convince them to occasionally include messages of faith in their posts in order to provoke an encounter with Christ or the Church among their friends and followers in the digital realm. This approach is in line with Pope Benedict XVI's consistent calls to evangelize the "digital continent."

EVANGELIZING THE DIGITAL CONTINENT

"I ask you to introduce into the culture of this new environment of communications and information technology the values on which you have built your lives.

"In the early life of the Church, the great apostles and their disciples brought the Good News of Jesus to the Greek and Roman world. Just as, at that time, a fruitful evangelization required that careful attention be given to understanding the culture and customs of those pagan peoples so that the truth of the Gospel would touch their hearts and minds, so also today, the proclamation of Christ in the world of new technologies requires a profound knowledge of this world if the technologies are to serve our mission adequately.

"It falls, in particular, to young people, who have an almost spontaneous affinity for the new means of communication, to take on the responsibility for the evangelization of this digital continent. Be sure to announce the Gospel to your contemporaries with enthusiasm. You know their fears and their hopes, their aspirations and their disappointments: the greatest gift you can give to them is to share with them the Good News of a God who became man, who suffered, died and rose again to save all people.

"Human hearts are yearning for a world where love endures, where gifts are shared, where unity is built, where freedom finds meaning in truth, and where identity is found in respectful communion. Our faith can respond to these expectations: may you become its heralds!"[8]

— Pope Benedict XVI

If we as a Church are trying to bring the Good News of Jesus Christ to all people, the digital continent is a great place to invest our energies. In fact, digital outreach efforts can be seen now as a litmus test of whether a parish community is primarily focused on the mission of proclaiming the Good News with new people or whether it is primarily focused on maintenance and serving the needs of current parishioners.

The Church is not a membership organization that has a mission. The Church is a mission. The Church continues the mission with which Christ was entrusted by God the Father. The Church seeks to fulfill that mission by bringing Christ to people today and bringing people to Christ. Participation in the life of the Church is open to everyone. We are all called to help one another on a path of continual conversion, to be more and more the unique person God created us to be.

New media represents a great opportunity for the Church. It can certainly be used to "warm hearts" on the digital continent — of those that are currently engaged in the life of the Church and of those that are currently far away.

THE PRIMARY TARGET AUDIENCE OF THE CHURCH'S NEW EVANGELIZATION EFFORTS

When the Church uses the word "evangelization," it normally means bringing the Good News about Jesus Christ to those unfamiliar with Christianity. We can think of the French and Spanish Catholic missionaries who came to America in the past several centuries and the many missionary orders that go to remote areas of the globe today.

We are now hearing the term "New Evangelization" more often in the United States and throughout the West. In this New Evangelization effort, the Church's target audiences are inactive Catholics, infrequent Catholics, and even those who consider themselves ex-Catholics. These Catholics have heard the name of Jesus Christ, perhaps received catechesis when they were young, and might be able to tell you many facts about Christ and the Church. Their hearts, however, are not burning with the love and friendship of Christ, warmed by the outreach of the Church, or nurtured regularly by the grace of the sacraments.

Jesus had a simple name in the Scriptures for followers in these situations — the lost. In the 15th chapter of the Gospel of St. Luke, Jesus tells us three parables in response to the grumblings of the Pharisees and scribes who did not like that he was spending time with sinners and tax collectors.

He first tells us the parable of the lost sheep. We see how the shepherd leaves the 99 to reach out and find the *one* that is lost. He tells us in this parable that the shepherd will *rejoice* when he finds the one. Jesus then adds, "There will be more joy in heaven over one sinner who repents than over ninety-nine righteous persons who need no repentance" (Lk 15:3-7).

Jesus then shares with us the parable of the lost coin, in which the woman searches for a lost silver coin, which likely could have come from a matrimonial headpiece, something that would be similar to someone today losing a wedding ring. When she finds it, she invites her neighbors to celebrate with her because she has found the coin she had lost. Then Jesus notes, "Just so, I tell you, there is joy before the angels of God over one sinner who repents" (Lk 15:8-10).

Finally, Jesus tells the parable of the prodigal son. We know the story well. When the son who disowned the family and squandered half the estate returns home, the loving father sprints out to meet him and then throws a huge party! To the older, faithful, jealous brother, the loving father explains (to paraphrase the Scripture passage), "We *had* to celebrate and rejoice, for this brother of yours was dead and has begun to live, and was lost and has been found" (Lk 15:11-32).

Pope Francis has been encouraging us as a Church to go to the peripheries and margins of human existence to find those who are far from Christ and to invite them home to Christ and the Church. This is a new way to express what Jesus called us to do not once or twice but *three times* in Luke 15, presumably in order to make sure we understood. The way Jesus ends each of the three parables is significant: we are told that there will be a *huge party* when ONE sinner returns to the family of Christ, which is the Church.

My hope is that the approaches and ideas in this book will provoke parishes to invite their parishioners to embrace new media as a way for the Church to be present in the community and to ask each parishioner to utilize a percentage of their messages (perhaps a tithe of 10 percent of their social media posts) to promote an encounter with Christ or the Church.

The request initially would be to invest the energy, prayer, and time needed to invite just one person who is away from the Church home and then to accompany that person on his or her journey, however long that might take. One way to do that would be to help parishioners envision the celebrations in heaven when one of the lost returns.

THE LOST — MUCH MORE THAN 1 PERCENT TODAY

Most parishioners, if prompted, could quickly list 10 or more Catholics close to them — relatives, neighbors, friends, co-workers, fellow students — who would fit the definition of "lost" from the Church.

Many parishes in the Northeast and Upper Midwest of the country, in fact, might be able to say something like this: "The majority of our parish and region is Catholic, but most of these Catholics do not come to Church. They do not know much about us, and we do not know much about them."

That statement is sad, but it is an unfortunate reality today in many neighborhoods that were once known for being strongly Catholic. In those same communities 60 years ago, the percentage of lost would have been much closer to the scriptural 1 of 100. Parishioners would know if someone missed Mass, and there would be visits to see if he or she were sick. Now Catholics that are away from Jesus the Good Shepherd in the sacraments outnumber those that are present for the Mass, the Shepherd's meal.

Matthew Kelly, in his 2012 book *The Four Signs of a Dynamic Catholic*, shared research that only 7 percent of Catholics are highly engaged in living their faith in their parishes, through prayer, study, generosity, and evangelization. This 7 percent is doing most of the work for the parish's ministries and providing most of the financial support. Kelly looks at this sobering statistic in an optimistic way, asking us to imagine the additional good we could do as a Catholic family if we could double the number of active parishioners to 14 percent over the course of the next several years.[9]

ENGAGING THE 93 PERCENT THROUGH NEW MEDIA

How can we engage the additional 93 percent in activities to allow them to encounter the Shepherd?

First, it helps to segment this group. There are those who attend Mass regularly but are not engaged in parish life outside of the Sunday Eucharist. We know in most parts of the country Mass attendance is between 15 and 35 percent typically. It is about 15 percent where I live. For the sake of discussion, let's say this group makes up about 20 percent of Catholics in America. Social media is one of several ways to connect the lost to the Church. Social media and email distribution lists could remind these people of parish events and opportunities to become more involved, to foster and deepen friendships with others in the community.

Then we have those who retain their identity as Catholics and come to Mass a couple of times a year. Perhaps they drop their children off at religious education on Sundays but do not choose to join the community at prayer. From their actions, we can classify them as infrequent. Surveys show that this group is about 40 percent of U.S. Catholics. Social media and email communication can share how participating actively in a faith community — through preaching, seminars, friendships, and service — is making a positive difference in parishioners' busy lives. Social media can make the Church more relevant, as they make choices on the weekend between Church and sleep, Church and sports, or Church and other activities that they are currently prioritizing. A first step is to get them to connect with us through these media platforms.

Finally we have "fallen away" or "ex-Catholics." This is about a third of all adults who were raised Catholic. Another way to look at this group is to consider that 10 percent of all adults in America are ex-Catholics.[10] Social media can be used to share articles, videos, and other links to stories that can be truly inspirational, to perhaps replace hurtful wounds and bad memories. Social media can also be used to remind them that the Church still exists to serve people in need and to share the helpful messages of Christ with a wounded world. Social media can convey that many people like them are happily involved in the life of the Church.

These group segmentations and the percentages do not matter as much as the fact that there are so many of our fellow Catholics that are lost from the Church today. We need a strategy and approaches that can reach those who are away.

The Power and Promise of New Media

New media can be a game changer for the Church in our outreach efforts because it is a tool to reach people who would otherwise not visit our churches and parish communities. It is also a great means to share the beauty of the Catholic faith through images, stories, and other links. We can help the non-engaged to direct their spiritual GPS on Christ and his loving invitation to the fullness of life, mercy, and the promises he has for those of us who choose to be his disciples.

I have five foundational beliefs that provide the reason for my hope in the promise of new media for evangelization:

1. **Every unengaged, inactive, or ex-Catholic in the United States can be connected with, or is just one digital message away from, at least ONE Catholic who is active and engaged through the various networks of social media.** This represents a huge opportunity. If parishes prioritize social media, we can establish and deepen those connections.

2. **Many engaged Catholics in the United States have never been asked or coached to see social media as a way to live out the Catholic faith and to reach out to those who are lost and hurting.** One reason for this is that parishes have not fully embraced social media themselves or become animators of the New Evangelization online.

3. **Motivating parishes and parishioners to prioritize outreach and evangelization is a challenge, but it is an easier sell today because of the use of new media by Pope Francis and the Vatican.** This motivation to reach the lost is a central part of the renewal Pope Francis is leading in the Church. We must help people at all levels of the Church to internalize that the lost are immensely important to Jesus and that he is immensely important to us. Therefore, should not those who are so important to him be also important to us? Should not his priority in finding the lost also be our priority, individually and collectively? Pope Francis' leadership in this area is encouraging not only pastors but also the faithful to follow his lead and not see social media as a fad.

4. **Catholics today are much more likely to be comfortable as digital missionaries, compared to using other forms of evangelization.** Social media, therefore, can be an outreach approach that can gain traction with our parishioners. The skills learned in sharing the beauty of our Catholic faith on social media will be transferable to personal one-on-one discussions too. Our parishioners today can be a new face of the Church, reflecting the divine face of Christ, to accompany those who are lost, one-by-one, to a new and deeper friendship with Christ and with the Catholic community.

5. **Parishes can train parishioners with the skills necessary to be effective digital missionaries.** My experience has taught me that most parishioners welcome this media training. This can be done through the formation of a New Media Outreach Commission, which would implement a series of initiatives over time.

Let's move on now, in the next chapter, to what recent popes have been writing and doing about how new media can be made a great place to encounter Christ and the Christian community. You may be struck by how passionate they are for evangelization through new media!

SUMMARY POINTS

- Pope Francis, like his predecessors, is calling for the Church to embrace the New Evangelization and to reach those who are on the margins and "lost," with the Gospel of Christ and with a fire of love that will warm others' hearts.

- The majority of Catholics today in the United States are "lost" from the Church to some extent (infrequent, inactive, or ex-Catholics).

- Social media can be a game changer for the Church. Those who are "lost" are likely connected on social media with Catholics who are engaged. Catholics on social media today, however, haven't been asked or coached to see social media as a way to live out their faith by reaching out to those who are lost and hurting. After receiving training and formation at their parish, Catholics are likely to be comfortable as digital missionaries, as a portion of their digital presence.

- A litmus test for whether a parish is engaged in mission or maintenance today is whether it sees itself as active in the culture and the communication flow of new media, because many of the "lost" spend large amounts of their life in the digital realm.

REFLECTION AND DISCUSSION QUESTIONS

In the territory of your parish, what percentage of the families are Catholic? Of this group, how many are actively engaged in parish life, infrequent, or not connected (in any visible way) with the parish community?

•••

Do you believe Jesus' words, in Luke 15, that heaven rejoices whenever one person who was lost returns to the Shepherd? If every Catholic acted as if this were literally true, how do you think that would transform the Church and transform everyone who participates in trying to bring someone home to the Church?

•••

Have you ever been heavily involved in accompanying someone to return to or to join the Catholic Church? How would you describe that experience to fellow parishioners, to encourage them to invite and accompany others home to our Catholic family?

Chapter Two

ENCOUNTERING CHRIST IN NEW MEDIA

"Dear Followers: I understand there are now over 10 million of you! I thank you with all my heart and ask you to continue praying for me."[11]

POPE FRANCIS, @PONTIFEX TWITTER ACCOUNT, OCTOBER 27, 2013

Parishes can learn a great deal from what our recent popes and the Vatican team responsible for social communications have been saying and doing in the area of new media.

Over the past few years, the Pontifical Council for Social Communications has helped Pope Benedict XVI and Pope Francis launch and grow News.va, a "mothership" website portal for current news; a mobile application called "ThePopeApp," which makes News.va content easily available on smartphones and tablets; a Facebook presence for News.va; and the @Pontifex Twitter account, in eight languages, which has grown to more than 10 million followers.

Chapter Two: Encountering Christ in New Media

In this chapter, I synthesize what I think are nine important insights that parishes and the entire Church can draw from what the popes and their collaborators in the Vatican have been saying in their messages and in their actions:

1. New media is here to stay; it is not a fad.

2. New media is a place where so many people spend significant portions of their lives — and if we're going to meet them, we have to be willing to meet them where they are.

3. The Church's presence in new media is substantive, symbolic, and transformative.

4. Through our presence on new media, the Church can reach people who would ordinarily not hear the Gospel.

5. The Church needs to understand new media's different culture and language and to immerse itself in it.

6. The Church's approach to new media should be to listen, to converse, to invite, and then to share its message.

7. New media is a great place for all people, including active Catholics, to learn more about the Church and grow in faith.

8. New media is a place of real encounter with the Church and with Christ.

9. The Church can be, and should be, the world's largest social network, connecting parishes across the globe.

1. NEW MEDIA IS HERE TO STAY; IT IS NOT A FAD

Monsignor Paul Tighe, the Irish secretary (second-in-command) of the Pontifical Council for Social Communications (PCCS), has indicated that after Pope Benedict XVI started using Twitter to spread the faith, the Vatican received many messages from dioceses across the world stating that the pope's action helped them to see that social media is not a fad but a serious forum of communication that is not going to go away.[12] Since it is a priority for the pope, they concluded that it should therefore be a priority at the local level of the Church.

The fact that there has been such a large and overwhelmingly positive response to the pope's tweets only serves to confirm that conclusion.

Monsignor Tighe has also spoken of the impact that Pope Francis' tweets (messages sent on Twitter) are making. His initial messages are delivered to accounts of his 14 million followers, and then many of those who receive those messages retweet (share or forward) them to their networks. Twitter has indicated that Pope Francis has one of the highest retweet rates of any significant account on Twitter. It is possible, therefore, that after those retweets arrive in people's accounts, Pope Francis' messages reach a sizable number of Twitter's 900 million users.

Despite Twitter messages being only 140 characters, the Vatican is showing that Scripture verses and teachings of the Church can be shared and introduced in a meaningful way by using that format. Also, because the tweets are powerfully written, they have also influenced newspaper headlines for some of Pope Francis' homilies, statements, and prayer services, such as the one that encouraged the world to pray for peace in Syria in September 2013.

While acknowledging that social media platforms — such as Twitter, Facebook, and YouTube — might have different levels of usage in 10 years, as new platforms continually get introduced, Vatican leaders are emphasizing that social media, in general, is here to stay, as an environment to exchange ideas and witness to our faith.

2. New Media Is a Place Where So Many People Spend Significant Portions of Their Lives — and If We're Going to Meet Them, We Have to Be Willing to Meet Them Where They Are

Pope Benedict XVI spoke often of the digital continent as a place where people are spending significant portions of their time. Pope Francis has echoed these observations by saying that digital (new) media are an existential dimension of many lives: "The world of communications, more and more, has become an 'environment' for many, one in which people communicate with one another, expanding their possibilities for knowledge and relationship."[13]

The Church sees the digital arena primarily not as a type of technology but as a forum for human communication. It is a place where people expand their knowledge, form new relationships, and communicate with one another. Large gatherings and discussions take place virtually. If we as a Church seek to go out of ourselves and find those who are alienated, hurting, and alone (as Pope Francis is imploring us), we then must enter social media in order to dialogue with adults today and to understand their hopes, desires, doubts, and concerns.

People are longing for meaning, for friendship, and for contact. Many are living on the peripheries of existence, even in big and active cities. Social media can help foster connectedness and understanding, and therefore, it is not a surprise that it has grown so rapidly. It provides the potential for the Church to reach people everywhere, overcoming time, space, and language barriers, to offer them the friendship of those in the Christian community and our witness to the beauty of living a life centered on Christ.

3. The Church's Presence in New Media Is Substantive, Symbolic, and Transformative

As Catholics, we bring a life-changing and life-saving message to the realm of digital media. Those messages are as substantive as any other messages that one can communicate. We seek that the entire world will hear them. When we place a message in new media, it is accessible instantaneously to people next door and also around the world.

Pope Benedict, Pope Francis, and their collaborators in the Vatican also recognize that their presence on Twitter and in other media formats is also symbolic. It recognizes and appreciates Catholic communities and individuals who have been working in these digital areas, and it also encourages those not yet present. If the pope is present, leading the way in the digital frontier, should not all ministers and parishes with access to technology also be present there too?

Our presence also can transform the type of discourse and raise the tone of the discussion. If a faithful Catholic or a priest, deacon, or religious is present in a conversation, people may choose more respectful and civil ways to discuss ideas and to affirm those that are present. In bringing who we are as Catholics to the exchange, we can introduce questions and topics that might lead everyone to reflect on how we are utilizing our scarce time and resources to grow and to help others.

Many conversations on social media can be helped by the sharing of enduring wisdom, experience, and tradition, particularly on the aspects and behaviors of true friendship. By our respect, authenticity, concern, patience, and behaviors, people might feel drawn to us and be more open to discuss questions of faith.

4. THROUGH OUR PRESENCE ON NEW MEDIA, THE CHURCH CAN REACH PEOPLE WHO WOULD ORDINARILY NOT HEAR THE GOSPEL

If the Church isn't present in the digital world, we're going to be absent from the lives of many of our contemporaries, particularly younger people, who spend significant portions of their lives there.

When approached with the idea to go on Twitter in 2012, Pope Benedict asked Vatican communication officials simply whether it would be a way for the Gospel message to reach new people and invite them to the Christian community. His primary instinct and intuition was that this is truly Good News and that we want to share it with people in all possible ways.[14]

Pope Benedict embraced this new frontier of evangelization. The growth of @Pontifex in eight languages has continued with each tweet of Pope Francis. It is clearly helping Pope Francis' words to reach people who would not ordinarily receive messages from the Church. One example is the nearly 260,000 followers on the pope's Twitter account in Latin. The Vatican believes many of these are Latin teachers and students who are not necessarily Catholic.[15]

Archbishop Claudio Celli, the president of the Pontifical Council for Social Communications, often employs the image of scattering seeds to discuss digital media — one does not know where messages are going to end up or whether they will land on fertile or hostile ground. The possibility always exists that a word or message, rooted in the Gospel, is going to move somebody's heart.

The intersecting networks of social media provide a great opportunity for the Church also. Those on social media can interact with the friends of their friends and follow them or make direct connections. Platforms like LinkedIn are built around these interlinked networks of friendships. The simple presence of Catholic organizations and individuals on social media, along with our large networks of friendships and institutions, can allow people with whom we are linked to connect with the global and local networks of the Catholic Church.

5. The Church Needs to Understand New Media's Different Culture and Language and to Immerse Itself in It

Social media is a different culture of communication from how the Church has historically communicated.

The Church communicates texts well, such as encyclicals, letters, and interviews. While these methods remain important today, many people, including devout Catholics, are less likely to read long texts, favoring instead the presentation of materials in an interactive format that includes images and sounds to accompany the written word. If those are the formats that speak to people's heads, hearts, and souls today, then the Church needs to express herself in those ways too.

The Church has also taught the faith traditionally through preaching. The pulpit is a one-way communication channel — the priest talks and the congregation listens. Advances in communication, such as radio and television, have allowed Church preaching to reach larger audiences in powerful ways, but it is still a format where there are few presenters and many receivers of the information.

The forms of social media are different because they are an interactive and participative style of communication. When someone presents a reflection or an idea, and you are moved, you can comment your agreement or disagreement, or perhaps add an insight and then share it with others. Teaching in this format is best done when the teacher engages in the posted comments or questions, even though this takes time. Often these responses in social media are public, so the answers can influence far more people than simply the person who posed the question.

Social media is changing the way people form relationships, friendships, communities, and how they learn. Young people are expressing themselves, gathering information, and learning in significantly different ways today because of social media. They are establishing communities and friendships in new ways. We want to be part of their communities and have genuine friendships with them. So we must adapt our ways of bringing people to Christ and the Church.

Monsignor Tighe has spoken of the need for the Church's vocabulary in social media to be entry-level, so that people can understand it. Perhaps, after someone engages with us, we can help that person more deeply understand our concepts. Many words from theology or the study of the liturgy are not entry-level words — for example, evangelization, reconciliation, salvation, and incarnation — and we should never presume that people understand what these terms mean. These rich words can sound like jargon to many people today and therefore can be intimidating or not inviting.[16] As individuals, we should recognize that our social media posts should be entry-level expressions of our faith so that they resonate with a broad audience that might click on a link and then explore our faith more deeply.

6. The Church's Approach to New Media Should Be to Listen, to Converse, to Invite, and Then to Share Its Message

When I first started to explore new media, I thought it was mainly a new distribution channel — an additional way for the Church to share its messages. One could take an article, newsletter, picture, video, or podcast and put it on a website or blog and then share the link in Facebook and Twitter. Many digital immigrants who venture into the social media for the first time, I believe, make a similar mistake.

New media can certainly be used to distribute content, but this viewpoint misses the essential point of the interactivity and participatory nature of the culture of social media. We as a Church need to rethink our communication approaches, in order to be effective participants in social media. We must move beyond the paradigm of "the Church speaks, you listen" discussed above and adopt an approach that says, "Let us discuss an important question in society today and what the Church (and Sacred Scripture and Sacred Tradition) have to say about it."

Pope Francis encourages us to use social media first "to reveal a presence that listens, converses, and encourages. Allow yourselves, without fear, to be this presence, expressing your Christian identity as you become citizens of this environment. A Church that follows this path learns how to walk with everyone."[17]

He wants us to be digital citizens who understand this culture and live in it responsibly. He wants us, first, to listen; then to dialogue; and third, to encourage people and bring them hope. He hopes that we will see what others' concerns and wounds are and then walk with them as we try to address their concerns and heal their wounds. He wants us to see ourselves in social media as being on a journey with other pilgrims. All people are on this journey, and we must walk with them. We should not be way ahead of others or way behind them. We accompany them at their own pace.

7. New Media Is a Great Place for All People, Including Active Catholics, to Learn More About the Church and Grow in Faith

The technological advances of the new forms of media in the past decades allow Catholics to quickly explore, with the help of a search engine, Sacred Scripture, the *Catechism of the Catholic Church*, the Church Fathers, and the writings of the Doctors of the Church. We can also take virtual tours of most of the sacred sites of Christendom, study the best works of Christian art and music, and stay current on the latest information and formational messages. This is a tremendous blessing for those who want to grow in faith and share it with others. One example of this is that many priests in the United States now read a synopsis of Pope Francis' daily homily on News.va, when they arise to prepare for their parish's daily Mass.

There are also many websites, videos, and mobile applications that can help us pray, understand difficult scriptural passages or teachings, find answers to tough questions, explore the liturgy, hear recordings of moving talks and homilies, prepare for confession, get involved in Christian service, find Masses while traveling, study to earn degrees in ministry and theology, and so much more. Because videos, photos, and audio now accompany words, these digital resources can be much more immersive and powerful expressions of our faith.

New content and applications continue to be developed each year. It is fair to ask, however, how many Catholics are currently aware of these resources and are utilizing them to grow in faith. What can be done to encourage more of our brothers and sisters — whether they are active, inactive, infrequent, or former Catholics — to be aware of these tools?

Social media provides two great helps in our efforts to allow this great content to reach more people. First, we can share links to these resources with our networks, as a witness, indicating how these resources have made a positive impact on us. Because we are the messengers presenting this opportunity, people who might not otherwise click on the link might do so. Second, we can share this information in a way that fosters discussion that we can facilitate. Faith should never be solely an individual pursuit; it is best lived in community. That is as true in the digital world as it is in the non-digital world.

8. New Media Is a Place of Real Encounter With the Church and With Christ

The preparatory documents for the 2012 Synod on the New Evangelization stated that the "Christian faith is not simply teachings, wise sayings, a code of morality or a tradition. The Christian faith is a true encounter and relationship with Jesus Christ. Transmitting the faith means to create in every place and time the conditions which lead to this encounter between the person and Jesus Christ. The goal of all evangelization is to create the possibility for this encounter, which is, at one and the same time, intimate, personal, public and communal."[18]

The Church's efforts in new media go far beyond simply sharing the details of what we believe and the wonderful works Christians have done throughout time, out of love for God and others. Our purpose as messengers of the faith is to bring people to an encounter with the living God and to communicate his nearness to us. New media can be a bridge for this encounter.

As people of faith, we can see that the anxiety and restless hearts of the world are caused by a distance from, or absence of, God from their lives. God continually is seeking out each of us with a merciful and tender heart. We are called to help others to recognize the signs of that outreach, and social media is a good way for us to do that.

Each encounter with Christ is unique and personal. It is a grace-filled, life-giving, and mysterious encounter. Our primary task is to witness to that encounter in our lives, to help others to learn how to ask Christ to make himself known to them, to encourage them to form a personal friendship with Christ, and to grow closer to him through participation in the Church community. It is our privilege to bring people to Christ.

Social media can foster this culture of encounter for the Church, as it is a place of conversation and dialogue. It can reach the most isolated regions of the world and create community. It can foster connections, communication, and understanding between individuals and within communities. It can bring about a culture where others feel listened to, accepted, understood, encouraged, and loved. We want people today to see the Church as an initiator of all these good things, and social media can allow us to do that.

9. The Church Can Be, and Should Be, the World's Largest Social Network, Connecting Parishes Across the Globe

The Church is the largest network for spiritual and material good in the world. The more than one billion Catholics form nearly 3,000 dioceses and more than 200,000 parishes. These local communities pray together and work with one another to establish schools, hospitals, and health care centers, service agencies, and so many other ministries. Most of these institutions are connected through their bishop to the bishop of Rome, the pope. We are a universal Church, structured as a global community of local communities.

For this reason, the Church should also have the largest social network in the world. Parishes and parishioners can be connected with Catholics on every other continent. Social media also allows the great possibility of forming and defining new small communities, as it allows groups to form along interests, themes, and topics, across borders and time zones.

The Church is not yet the worldwide digital network it hopes to be. One way for the Church to connect its vast network of parishes, schools, health care centers, and agencies together online would be to implement the new domain dot-Catholic, which could replace or augment the dot-org, dot-net, or dot-com domain names currently used by most parishes today. The naming mechanism could be something like ParishnameTownname.Diocese.Catholic (envision St. Patrick's Cathedral in New York having a web address on this new top-level domain of www.SaintPatrickCathedral.NewYork.Catholic).

In terms of social media, parishes and other Catholic organizations can connect with universal social media accounts to receive and share information. Chapter Four, on parishes as hubs of new media, will discuss this in detail.

•••

Despite the calls to embrace new media, many parishes have been slow to embrace these transformational tools of Facebook, Twitter, YouTube, blogs, comment boxes, and smartphone apps, all of which are so heavily used by people of all ages, particularly young people. Why? We'll cover that in Chapter Three.

SUMMARY POINTS

- New media is here to stay; it is not a fad.

- New media is a place where so many people spend significant portions of their lives — and if we're going to meet them, we have to be willing to meet them where they are.

- The Church's presence in new media is substantive, symbolic, and transformative.

- Through our presence on new media, the Church can reach people who would ordinarily not hear the Gospel.

- The Church needs to understand new media's different culture and language and to immerse itself in it.

- The Church's approach to new media should be to listen, to converse, to invite, and then to share its message.

- New media is a great place for all people, including active Catholics, to learn more about the Church and grow in faith.

- New media is an environment of real encounter with the Church and with Christ.

- The Church can be and should be the world's largest digital network, connecting parishes across the globe.

REFLECTION AND DISCUSSION QUESTIONS

What are the most profound ways that new communication technologies are changing human interactions?

•••

How many people close to you live a significant portion of their lives on the digital continent? How would you like to see the Church be present to them?

•••

How have you been encouraged through tools of new media to grow in your Catholic faith?

•••

What hopes and concerns do you have for the Church as it expands its presence in new media? What concerns do you have personally in embracing new media and in sharing your faith through it?

Chapter Three

OVERCOMING FEARS AND OBSTACLES

"Go therefore and make disciples of all nations,
baptizing them in the name of the Father and of the
Son and of the Holy Spirit, teaching them to observe
all that I have commanded you; and behold, I am with
you always, to the close of the age."

MATTHEW 28:19-20

The messages from recent popes are clear, in that they wish the entire Church would embrace digital media for the sharing and spreading of the Gospel. To this point, however, there has been slow implementation of parishes worldwide. In this chapter, we look at the reasons for resistance here in the United States. For social media to fulfill its potential, we need to understand parish leaders' concerns, speak to them, and overcome them.

Change is hard. That is true in all types of organizations, including the Church. Every organization has established ways of doing things. We all can get comfortable with the routines. We get good at using current tools and processes to achieve good outcomes. There is a part in all of us that seeks to become the best we can be in our roles. Changing something significant, which causes us to learn an entirely new subject matter or skill, produces anxiety.

When I present a plan for change to a group, I expect to hear resistance. When it inevitably comes, I try to process whether it is due to a general hesitancy or rather to a strong rejection of the proposed change.

In the case of embracing social and digital media within the Church, the vast majority of the concerns expressed can be described as "hesitancy." Part of that is due to our population in the Church — not many of us are "innovators" or "early adopters" when it comes to technology. Many of us prefer to adopt technology later on, after it is proven.[19] In the language of the digital continent, as shared in the Introduction, we are more "digital immigrants" than "digital natives."

In addition to slowness in embracing of new technologies, however, some parishes also can be resistant to change longstanding communication methods.

In various meetings over the past few years, I have asked pastors and parish staff members about their attitudes, willingness, and reasons for adopting (or not adopting) technology. I ask questions such as, "Why do you think so few parishes have embraced this?" or "What do you think our office at the archdiocese can do to help parishes embrace this more quickly?" The responses have been intriguing.

Many of the explanations have to do with simply embracing change in general or adopting new technology. Here are some reasons given for the slow pace in adopting new technology.

CONCERNS ABOUT EMBRACING NEW TECHNOLOGY IN THE PARISH

1. We **lack the time** to learn it and then do it well. It is more work. Changing and learning is a lot of work. (*We do not see this as a high enough priority to adjust our schedules to make this happen.*)

2. We **lack the money** to implement this. Our budget is already stretched. *(We do not see this as a high enough priority to adjust the budget to make this happen.)*

3. We **lack the expertise** in the parish office to do this. We do not really understand all this technology. *(We do not see this as a high enough priority to gain the expertise to do this well.)*

4. This is **not the right time** to take on something new. We are **exhausted** trying to keep up with all the things we do. *(We do not see this as a high enough priority to "make time" for this.)*

5. We are **satisfied with the way we currently do things**. The status quo works for our parishioners and staff. *(We are comfortable with our routines and habits. We are focused more on our current parishioners' needs than those of the "lost.")*

6. We have **tried and failed before** when we have implemented similar new things. We do not want to fail again. *(We want to be competent and skilled at everything we do.)*

7. We do not understand **how this will make us a stronger parish**. Is it just to "appear modern?" *(What is the reward for investing the time and the risk? When it is proven elsewhere, maybe we will give it a shot.)*

8. We should **consult others before we do this**. *(We do not feel comfortable making this decision on our own. Referring it for further consultation is a polite way of saying no.)*

9. We should **only do this if we can do it well**. We'll turn people away if it is not excellent. So let's wait until it is proven and all the problems have been worked out. *(We are "late adopters," not "early adopters." Let some other parish make the mistakes and lead the way.)*

10. We'll **become much more dependent on others** outside the parish office to run and troubleshoot the technology. That is a concern. *(It can be scary to give up our autonomy and control.)*

11. **Our active parishioners are critical of most change efforts.**
    *(Change is hard and scary sometimes, as it takes us out of our
    comfort zone. It requires effort to prepare and to lead. It forces us
    to deal with complaints — who wants to deal with complaints?)*

SOME CONCERNS EXPRESSED ABOUT EMBRACING NEW MEDIA

1. **This is a fad.** We'll do it after everyone else (particularly the
   diocese) does it. *(The bishop hasn't asked the central ministries
   of the diocese to embrace this in a big way, and most of the larger
   parishes around us have not adopted this either. Shouldn't they do
   it first? If it is not a priority at the diocesan level, should it really be
   one at the parish level?)*

2. **This will not work as an outreach strategy.** This is just another
   form of communication with the same people. *(We do not need
   it. With the time that must be invested, what are the benefits? We
   have seen no convincing data that proves this will work. Where are
   the examples of other parishes where this has worked?)*

3. **This might divide the parish, as we'll leave people behind.**
   Many of our active parishioners are not on social media, and it
   will make them feel excluded. *(Some parishioners are not even on
   email. We are concerned that if active parishioners feel excluded,
   then it will hurt their engagement and contributions. It will also
   lead to complaints, because social media might change the nature
   of the relationship between the parish and our parishioners, between parishioners with one another, and change the demographic
   and spiritual makeup of the parish. Why risk it?)*

4. **It is the wrong strategy to grow the Church.** Our Church has
   the magisterium, as well as a hierarchy of authority and truths,
   and social media flattens that hierarchy. *(The forms of social
   media are popular with young people because they adopt many
   norms of youth culture. These are more than communication tools;
   they involve cultural change. Most of our parishioners are not in
   that generation and have concerns about young peoples' values
   that are often "spiritual, not religious." Now that we are in the
   post-sexual-abuse era, shouldn't we be practicing the forms of tra-*

ditional communication that are established, safe, and controlled? There are too many risks.)

5. **We do not understand it.** How is social media making a positive difference in the world? *(Is not social media just for gossip? Does it not principally involve self-absorbed, pushy, and narcissistic people posting information about trivial things going on in their life? Shouldn't we as a Church want to advocate face-to-face and personal relationships over social media?)*

6. **This is not a good use of limited pastoral resources.** We can only do so much. There is no one on our staff, besides our youth minister, with the skills for this. *(It is out of the comfort zone for most of our staff and will create extra work for each of us. Establishing it is only the first step, then we will need to continue to post content, read what others post, and engage in dialogue. It is a burden and a responsibility to monitor the activity and to do this well. It is hard enough to keep up with emails. How do we respond to everyone who connects with us through these new tools?)*

7. **It doesn't fit ME (as a minister) well.** I prefer to be intentional and deliberate, and this is not for me. *(I am not a networker, nor am I comfortable with this new technology that calls me to be a social networker. This is for the next generation of parish leaders. I am too tired and old to take this on now.)*

Underlying all of these reasons is a context that parish life is hard today, particularly compared to three or four decades ago, when there were more vocations, more Mass attendees, more money, more engagement, and fewer problems.

Given this context, it is easy to understand why many leaders see digital media as "more work." Because it is new, and since there are few well-publicized stellar examples thus far of Catholic parishes seeing great results, it is also easy to understand why parish leaders would be hesitant to invest the time and personnel resources to do this well, to become a leader, to deal with staff or parishioner complaints, or to envision changes to staff duties (or even the paid roles on the staff) to adjust to the communication patterns of younger and newer parishioners today. It is natural to avoid the risk of failure if success has not been proven elsewhere. Realistically, few will complain if we do not embrace it; more will complain, however, if we do.

OVERCOMING THE HESITANCY THROUGH IDENTIFYING THE CULTURAL RESISTANCE

How can we overcome all these reasons for hesitancy and resistance? While there are many concerns, it doesn't seem that any are too large to overcome if a big enough reason to implement new media becomes apparent.

What is that big enough reason? Perhaps we should start by consolidating all of the reasons above into a root explanation. My belief is that the biggest and most inclusive reason Catholic parishes have not embraced new media is because their *culture* and the main activities are preoccupied with **maintenance** (or **survival**) instead of **mission**. *Social media outreach is fundamentally a mission activity, not a survival or maintenance one.* The more that parishes embrace mission, the more they will embrace new media as a tool for outreach and evangelization.

In his 2005 book, *From Maintenance to Mission: Evangelization and the Revitalization of the Parish*, Father Robert Rivers, C.S.P., indicates that the Second Vatican Council was centered on evangelization and that many parishes four decades later still have not embraced evangelization as their central mission. He encouraged parishes to move from a maintenance mind-set (in which the primary target audience for parish ministries is current parishioners) to a mission mind-set, in which parishes are called to outreach, to seek and find the lost and those away from the Church.[20]

EXPERIENCE OF CHURCH OF THE NATIVITY

Father Michael White and Tom Corcoran, in their 2013 book, *Rebuilt: Awakening the Faithful, Reaching the Lost, Making Church Matter*, were blunt and direct in describing typical parish culture today. They write that "**demanding consumers**" dominate most parish cultures and that parish staffs have catered to the demands and preferences of their main "customers," their active parishioners. This was certainly true of their parish, Nativity, in Timonium, Maryland, in the Archdiocese of Baltimore.

In some places, parish life has become a membership club instead of a movement. Comfort is preferred to mission. Growth, expressed in spiritual advancement of individual members, or outreach to help make new disciples, simply is not a priority. Parishioners look to the parish staff as employees instead of spiritual guides and catalysts. The work of evangelization, of making disciples, is always thought to be someone else's job or something that we will get to when we have more time, financial resources, and extra help. It is seldom a top priority of the parish or of particular families. **Evangelization, through *any* tool or approach, is currently not a "must-do" activity**.[21]

If Father White and Corcoran are correct that evangelization is not currently the first priority for some parishes, it is easy to see why these parishes also have not embraced social media to allow for more effective evangelization. I believe that many parishes have never made an intentional choice to avoid evangelization activities but that **many parishes would describe evangelization as important but not urgent** in the way they allocate their time and budget. Evangelization is the type of activity we intend to get to but never find the time to do.

When evangelization becomes both an important and urgent thing to do, a top priority of a parish, the results can be fantastic. Father White and Corcoran describe in *Rebuilt* how they changed the culture of their parish through focusing all parishioners on reaching the "lost" and developing a strategy to foster spiritual growth for all those in their parish (old and new). Their vision became "make Church matter by growing disciples *who are growing disciples* among dechurched Catholics in north Baltimore and influencing churches to do the same elsewhere." Their mission statement, taken from Matthew 22 and Matthew 28 came to be, simply, "Love God, love others, make disciples."

Nativity's principal strategy is to present the life-changing Gospel message in a fresh and relevant way. They do this through a comprehensive "weekend experience" of Mass with music, message and ministries working together to make it an irresistible experience for newcomers, as well as weekend programs for kids and students, wherein the challenging formational messages parallel the adult homilies. They encourage all parishioners to serve at least once per month in a parish ministry and also to join a small group within the parish to grow in their faith and fellowship.[22] Not surprisingly, the Church of the Nativity is active on the digital continent, with an online campus, strong websites, as well as email, Twitter, and Facebook outreach.

Rebuilt describes the often painful process of cultural change within the Church of the Nativity to become more focused on the mission of evangelization. By articulating that parishioners seek to become "growing disciples *who are growing disciples*" through their outreach, service, small groups, prayer, and weekend experiences, Nativity has seen remarkable fruits, including a tripling of Mass attendance, spiritual growth, small-group momentum, dramatically increased giving, and greatly expanded volunteering and service. What parish community would not want these results?

Nativity's parishioners were inspired to become growing disciples. They understood that to be a growing disciple, each one had to take action to grow his or her own faith, as well as that of others. Cardinal Seán O'Malley in the Foreword put it this way: "A good indicator of whether we are evangelized is whether we, in turn, are evangelizers." Nativity's parishioners understand that a very important part of living as a disciple is to reach out to others in order to invest in them, to invite them to participate in a loving community, and then to journey alongside them all the way to heaven.

How can a parish best activate its parishioners to do this? We'll discuss that next in Chapter Four.

SUMMARY POINTS

- Overall, the Church has been hesitant to embrace new media. We discuss many reasons for this. Part of the slow response might be resistance to change in general, where parishes believe they lack the expertise, time, money, energy, motivation, and compelling rationale to do this well. Part of the slow response is also due to resistance to the idea of social media, believing that it is a fad that will not work as an outreach strategy, may leave some parishioners behind, doesn't fit with Church culture, and is outside the comfort zone of many parish staff members.

- The biggest reason, however, that new media has not been adopted fully at many parishes is cultural. Evangelization (reaching the lost, inviting them to become growing disciples in a community) is not acted upon as the top priority and central mission of the parish because parishes are in maintenance mode (or survival mode) and because many parishioners act as "demanding consumers," instead of evangelized evangelizers.

REFLECTION AND DISCUSSION QUESTIONS

How would you describe the culture and main activities of your parish? Do you think you are in mission mode or more in maintenance mode? How central is evangelization and outreach to your parish culture?

•••

What approach would you recommend for engaging parishioners in your parish in the task of outreach and evangelization?

•••

Where would outreach and evangelization rank in your household's activities and priorities? Your individual activities and priorities?

Chapter Four

PARISHES: ANIMATING HUBS FOR CATHOLIC NEW MEDIA

"We cannot keep ourselves shut up in parishes, in our communities, when so many people are waiting for the Gospel!"[23]

Pope Francis, @Pontifex Twitter account, July 27, 2013

In the parable of the lost sheep, Jesus instructs all his disciples — us — that central to being a student and follower of Christ is to seek the "lost." We are called by him, in Matthew 28:19-20, to "go" and "make disciples" of all people, "baptizing them in the name of the Father and of the Son and of the Holy Spirit," and then "teaching them to observe all" that he has commanded and taught us, so that they can become growing disciples who, in turn, seek the lost.

What Is the Parish and What Is It Called to Do?

The parish is the place where most Catholics experience the Church. Some Catholics mistakenly refer to the "parish" as the Church building(s). Others think about the parish as simply parish leadership or just the pastor himself. But the parish really is a community, a family, of all of us who join together to worship God in a particular area.

Canon law defines the parish as the "community of the Christian faithful" established on a stable basis within "a particular church [a diocese]."[24] The *Catechism of the Catholic Church* adds that parishes are "the place where all the faithful can be gathered together for the Sunday celebration of the Eucharist. The parish initiates the Christian people into the ordinary expression of the liturgical life: it gathers them together in this celebration; it teaches Christ's saving doctrine; it practices the charity of the Lord in good works and brotherly love."[25]

The Church is all of us, gathered to celebrate the Eucharist and sent out to the world. The word for Mass comes from the Latin word *missa*, which means, "to be sent on a mission." The Eucharist nourishes us and unites us with the Lord so that we can accomplish the mission Christ has given to the Church universal and to each of us.

Practicing the Spiritual and Corporal Works of Mercy

Catholics can often minimize the "good works and brotherly love" the *Catechism* speaks of to be only the corporal works of mercy, those that care for material and bodily needs. The Catholic Church has led the way in the United States in so many ministries of feeding the hungry, providing clothes and shelter, caring for the sick, and visiting those in prison. Institutionally, Catholics have formed inspiring ministries, such as Catholic Charities, Society of St. Vincent de Paul, Catholic Relief Services, health care, orphanages, meal centers, food pantries, shelters, and cemeteries.

Given the rampant secularism in this age, however, in addition to continuing those good works, we must also practice with as much fervor the spiritual works of mercy, those that care for the soul. Together, as one Catholic family, we can first do more to teach the uninformed, counsel the doubtful, help people turn from sinful to virtuous behavior, bear wrongs patiently, forgive offenses willingly, comfort the afflicted, and pray for the living and the dead. We want to invite them first to become disciples and then encourage and help them to become *growing* disciples. We desire to reach out to those who have been already baptized and have received some Catholic formation, but who have drifted away from the Church, and to encourage them to reconnect and grow more deeply in their acknowledgment of God's love and will in their lives. This is the work of the New Evangelization.

FOCUSING ON THE LOST

Pastors, priests, and parish staff by themselves can only reach a small fraction of those lost to the Church. As parishioners, perhaps without reflecting on it, we can sometimes treat parish staff as "employees," whose outreach we support through the parish collection. Stated another way, we can look at parish staff members as a consumer would, instead of as a disciple. Our parish staff members and leaders certainly need to model and lead the work of the entire parish to be a growing community of growing disciples, but it is up to every one of us to do the work of inviting people back to the Church.

We all can increase our efforts at outreach. Pastors in the Archdiocese of Boston have stated in seminars I have led that about 95 percent of their work is directed to serving the needs of current parishioners, with only about five percent focused on reaching out to non-parishioners. They have indicated that the percentage of time focused on evangelization needs to increase and that the minimal time they are spending at outreach is likely more than most of their parishioners.

When the entire parish community is mobilized, we can reach thousands of our neighbors and friends. If we utilize social media to do this, one parish can probably reach millions, due to the reach of our social networks. Should reaching thousands of people lost from the Church, with a message of invitation and welcome, be a monthly goal of each parish?

PARISHES AS *ANIMATORS* AND PARISHIONERS AS *AGENTS* OF THE NEW EVANGELIZATION

In October 2012, bishops from throughout the world gathered in Rome for the 13th Ordinary Synod of Bishops, which corresponded to the beginning of the Church's Year of Faith. The title of the synod was "The New Evangelization for the Transmission of the Christian Faith." In its final propositions, reflecting Catholic theology and the remarks shared by bishops and invited experts, the synod concluded that the "parish, in and through all of its activities, should animate its members to become agents of the New Evangelization, witnessing through both their words and their lives."[26]

Let's study and break down this proposition.

The parish, both **in** its activities and **through** its activities, is designed to accomplish something. We grow as disciples when we participate *in* parish activities — such as liturgy, prayer, adult-formation programs, service ministries, and parish-based outreach efforts. We also grow as disciples when *through* parish activities we become mobilized to act as Catholic followers of Christ in the world.

The synodal bishops want parishes, through these activities, to **animate** parishioners — that is, to be full of life, specifically the life Christ offers us and hopes we accept. People who are animated have energy, passion, enthusiasm, and love for what they do.

Parishes are specifically called to animate parishioners to be **agents of the New Evangelization**. Agents are people who act, often with the power entrusted by someone else, to act on another's behalf. We think, for example, of a sports agent who represents an athlete in negotiations with a professional team or to secure a product-endorsement contract. We, as Christ's followers, are also called to be his agents — his arms, legs, voices, ambassadors — to all those individuals and groups whom he has placed in our lives, to be his instrument in their salvation. What a privilege this is.

How are we called to be Jesus' agents? Through **witnessing**, through our **words** and our **lives**. When we witness, we share in a personal way that we have encountered an event, a person, and an experience. As Christians, we share our encounter with the person of Jesus Christ and the grace-filled encounters we experience through the Church that Christ founded. We are called to do this in two ways

— verbally and through our actions, especially how we live. St. Francis of Assisi has been the inspiration for the saying, "Preach always, and when necessary, use words." The way we live our lives — caring for others and building a civilization of love in our neighborhoods, workplaces, communities, and parishes — will "preach" to all those we encounter what we, and our faith, are about.

MATTHEW KELLY, FROM DYNAMICCATHOLIC.COM, ON THE NEED FOR A GAME CHANGER

"When 70% of Catholics don't go to church on Sunday, isn't it time someone did something? **We think it is.**

"The tide is going out on Catholicism in America. Catholics are leaving the Church at an alarming rate, and disengagement among those who remain is staggeringly high. Growing numbers of Catholics are disillusioned, questioning their faith, and filled with doubts about the modern relevance of Catholicism. Dwindling Mass attendance, scarcity of vocations, and Catholic school closures are just a few of the signs.

"The sad truth is that most Catholics have never really been shown the genius of Catholicism and how it could animate their lives.

"Business as usual will not turn the tide. In fact, business as usual will not even stem the tide. We need to start thinking on a whole new level. We need game changers.

"**Our response [at Dynamic Catholic]:** We believe that millions of ordinary Catholics want to be involved in a movement that provides a game-changing strategy for the Church today.

"We are passionate about finding a way for every Catholic to play a role in the great renewal that everyone knows the Catholic Church desperately needs."[27]

MANY PARISHES NEED A "GAME CHANGER" TO BOOST THEIR EFFORTS AT THE NEW EVANGELIZATION

Many parishes today need a game changer — one approach, attitude, or shift — that can significantly change the trajectory of our outreach and evangelization activities.

How can we help active Catholics today to **share** more often the generous and free gift of Jesus Christ's saving love for each of us? Imagine what would happen if every Catholic looked for each opportunity to discuss Jesus' unconditional love to everyone he or she cares about. That is the "business" the Church is in — proclaiming the Good News of Jesus Christ and helping people to reconcile it with reason, their lived experiences, and the prevailing culture.

Embracing social media within the parish and encouraging all parishioners to utilize it well can be a game changer. Envision what would be the impact if every parish's culture and approach activated *all* parishioners (young, old, and everyone in between) to learn social media skills and utilize social media as a tool to build more and deeper relationships — and then, within those relationships, to share experiences of faith. The reach can be far broader and have more impact than even what the Church of the Nativity experienced in Timonium, Maryland.

A small parish anywhere in the United States could reach **hundreds of thousands** simply by sharing messages using social media networks in a way that their friends could share and reshare (through "likes" and "retweets") their posts. These could be messages of invitation, opportunities to discuss how to overcome some of life's challenges, or links to a compelling presentation of the Church's perspective on some of life's biggest questions. One parish community could transform an area far larger than its parish territory.

New media platforms can also streamline and improve ongoing communications to those who are currently parishioners, for helping them to grow in the knowledge of their faith, update on programs, and more. As with most things Catholic, new media outreach is a "both/and" approach; it reaches both those who are lost and those who are already found.

New media outreach is also a force multiplier, as content and messages can be shared with minimal effort and no cost. The value of a simple message shared by a friend is of interest to you because it is *your* friend who shared it.

PARISHES — HUBS OF NEW MEDIA ACTIVITY

When I began writing this book, I confess that I thought the key goal was to get parishes to embrace digital media for themselves, and to be "agents" of new media, so that parish ministers could better engage, connect with, and foster dialogue within the existing group of parishioners and help them grow as disciples. In some ways, a parish that had a great new media program was the "end."

As I reflected further, I became convinced that parishes on new media platforms are not an "end" but a "means to the end." For the Church to be fully alive, for the Church to be living the sacred mission to which Christ calls us, **I now believe that the goal is for individual Catholics to become the "agents" of new media** — being present on the new media platforms, witnessing to their lives, inviting others to (re)connect with our Catholic community — and that parishes need to be the "animators" to help them get there.

A "wow" moment for me came when I thought about the various strategies parishes can use to truly animate parishioners to be agents of the New Evangelization today. I envisioned three possible parish-based, Monday-evening seminars directed toward engaging parishioners in the New Evangelization. All three options involve the work of evangelization and could bear fruit. Which one would attract the greatest attendance and engage the parishioners to become active agents?

- Seminar 1: Come learn how to conduct a successful door-to-door neighborhood outreach.

- Seminar 2: Come learn how to invite family members and friends back to the Church when you see them at Thanksgiving and Christmas.

- Seminar 3: Come learn how to utilize Twitter and Facebook to connect with old friends, communicate more often with family members, and learn a lot about your favorite subjects.

Seminars 1 and 2 are very important activities and would attract some parishioners. It is my clear opinion, however, that Seminar 3 would significantly outdraw the first two because the personal benefits for the parishioner are greater and the fears are likely to be fewer.

Social media participation is something that parishioners will want to do for reasons beyond the task of evangelization. If someone they trust in the parish teaches them how to sign up for social media, make connections (to family, friends, colleagues, fellow parishioners, and important organizations), use it well, and begin new conversations, this could be of great help to them. The benefits of increased communication within relationships and new sources of friendship become very clear almost immediately. This is a great service to parishioners.

As described in Chapter Two, Pope Francis (and Pope Benedict XVI before him) is calling each of us to embrace the digital continent, spend time on it, and become good citizens there — similar to the way we bring a Christian heart to physical neighborhoods and communities. From experience, we know that we are nourished by our relationships, and we like to be surrounded by good people who can become dependable friends and whom we can assist when they need our help. This is also true in social media.

Many of us have been formed throughout our lives — in our families, schools, religious education programs, and workplaces — to build effective relationships and to care for the needs of others through in-person encounters, phone conversations, correspondence, and more recently, through email. Parish-based outreach makes a great difference in serving the needy in most local areas.

It is true, however, that large numbers of the lost — those the Good Shepherd wants us to reach and invite to come home to the Church — live many hours of their day on the digital continent. Often, the "witnesses" they might otherwise value — friends from the "old neighborhood" or from high school or college, or even new friends, wherever they live now — are not readily available to meet in person. Reconnecting with such friends or family members through brief encounters on social media platforms is an effective way to build relationships, to strengthen friendships, and to share our faith in God.

Once parishioners are established on the digital continent, parishes can show them to how to use it for outreach on behalf of the Church community. Initial messages could simply be checking in when they are at Mass, or that they are looking forward to an evening seminar, or posting how the Sunday homily challenged them. From there, they may graduate to inviting a friend to get involved in a service-ministry event or attend a parish supper. A parish can ask those already using social media to commit to "tithing" 10 percent of their social media messages to be faith based (more on this later).

What must a parish do to be an effective and animating new media hub? We'll discuss many practical strategies throughout this book, but a key one is to think about how hubs serve the airline industry. Airport hubs are places that receive flights from most everywhere, and they allow passengers to be effectively redirected to other locations ("spokes") on a second flight.

In a similar way, parishes can receive high quality Catholic posts, blogs, and articles and then redistribute them to parishioners who are connected with them on social media, and in turn (through education, encouragement, and appreciation) those parishioners would share those messages (through liking, retweeting, emailing, etc.) with all their families and friends. One parish staff member or volunteer can effectively do this in less than 30 minutes a day — and the messages could reach millions. Diocesan new media offices can recommend a list of good sources of Catholic information. News agencies in Rome provide great materials to share with your parishioners. (See Appendix V — "Connecting Parishioners With the Universal Church and Helpful Catholic Resources" — and ParishGuideToNewMedia.com for a list of resources.)

THE POWERFUL REACH OF SOCIAL MEDIA

A short hypothetical example of the exponential power of social media's reach can illustrate this point.

Imagine that Holy Apostles Parish sent out this tweet: **"Wow! Pope Francis to visit Holy Apostles Parish in September 2015. Please retweet. #PopeVisit2015."**

Assume that the parish has 500 parishioners on Twitter, each of its parishioners has the average number of followers on Twitter

(208 in mid-2013) and each of their followers respectively has 208 followers.

- The *first* generation of the tweet would reach the 500 parishioners on Twitter.

- The *second* generation: If 25 percent of parishioners retweet that message, the second generation of the tweet would reach 26,000 (500 x 0.25 x 208).

- The *third* generation: If 10 percent of those who receive the second-generation message retweet it, it would reach 540,800 (26,000 x 0.1 x 208).

- The *fourth* generation: If 5 percent of those who receive the third-generation message retweet it, it would reach 5,624,320 (540,000 x 0.05 x 208).

In this hypothetical example, this message could reach a total of 5,624,320, even when a small percentage of those receiving the message share it. There will inevitably be some overlap of networks, so the above numbers are likely higher than they would be in reality. The main point, however, is simply to show how one powerful tweet in one parish could reach millions!

Animators of New Media

To become ***animators*** of new media, not just agents, parishes must embrace new media first so that reluctant parishioners can follow their lead. Parishes can train and educate parishioners in social media tools and facilitate the discussion of best practices in how to utilize them. Parishes can teach and preach that the main mission of the Church is to reach the lost, and encourage parishioners to think of themselves as disciples who are sent. They can use techniques that make it easy for parishioners to share faith-related messages provided by the parish or other places recommended by the parish or diocese.

Parish communications will truly transform and contribute to the growth of the Church when parishioners receive parish messages, internalize them, and share them with the world. If a parish is truly committed to evangelization as a priority, social media outreach is a high-potential approach. Someone might say, "That sounds like a lot of work. What is the best way for the parish to do all of this?" We will discuss the best ways to do this in our next chapter.

SUMMARY POINTS

- Parishes are called to be centers of evangelization and to reach the lost in their communities. The 2012 synod on "The New Evangelization for the Transmission of the Christian Faith" stated that parishes should become *animators* and parishioners *agents* of the New Evangelization.

- Unfortunately, many parishes and parishioners today only spend a minimal amount of their time on the task of evangelization. With 70 percent or more of Catholics not coming to church and many other unchurched, atheists, and agnostics in our communities, there are many people we can be reaching with invitations to join us in conversation and community.

- The Church needs a "game changer" to spark the New Evangelization. New media, coupled with strong faith, can be that game changer.

- As a hub for Catholic new media, parishes can catalyze the spiritual growth of active parishioners and serve as the center of a "hub-and-spoke" network of connected Catholics to share short messages about our faith with their networks and, through their friends' networks, with a sizable portion of the local community. This hub-and-spoke network of parishioner outreach can propel a parish's vision to be a truly "growing community of growing disciples."

- It is important that parishes lead the way in new media and animate this electronic outreach by receiving social media communications, sharing them with parishioners and asking parishioners to extend the reach of the parish through their own social media, making it easy to reach tens of thousands (or more) with each thoughtful message. The parish, working with its diocesan new media office, is an important hub of authentication of good Catholic content.

REFLECTION AND DISCUSSION QUESTIONS

What percentage of your extended family, friends, work colleagues, and neighbors are Catholic but not living as active disciples, particularly by not participating regularly in Sunday Mass?

•••

Are you active in social media? Why or why not? If so, which organizations and individuals do you follow and how did you find them?

•••

How would you maximize participation and attendance at a training session on social media in your parish?

•••

How can your parish best become an animator of the New Evangelization? What would be your top "game-changing" approach to help parishioners embrace the role as agents of the New Evangelization?

Chapter Five

LAUNCHING A NEW MEDIA OUTREACH INITIATIVE

"Let us remember that faith is not something we possess, but something we share. Every Christian is an apostle."[28]

POPE FRANCIS, @PONTIFEX TWITTER ACCOUNT, JULY 18, 2013

Your parish now understands that it has been asked by Pope Francis, as the Vicar of Christ, to reach out to those who inhabit the digital continent. You understand the reasons, and obstacles, why many parishes have not done it yet but have concluded that, if evangelization and outreach is truly a "must-do" activity, then your parish will figure a way to make this happen. You recognize that for parish communications to be truly transformative for parishioners and newcomers, and for those communications to foster the growth of the Church, then parishes must see themselves as hubs of new media activity. Parishes must animate their parishioners to become agents of the New Evangelization by receiving parish messages and sharing them with their friends and networks through new media.

Where should a parish begin? First, I recommend a day of prayer and reflection for key pastoral team leaders. For this day to realize its potential to transform the lives of tens, hundreds, or thousands, it needs to be rooted in prayer and formulated (and customized for your particular environment) under the guidance of the Holy Spirit.

Two of the key things to pray for are the courage and the energy to get the process started. Another is to identify which leaders within the parish community should be involved at the beginning, in organizing and planning. A third is to beg the Holy Spirit for the gifts to recognize obstacles, the perseverance to overcome them, and protection for these evangelization tasks.

One outcome from this prayer and reflection should be a plan regarding whom to approach to do the early work of establishing the initiative. At this stage, one to three staff members or parishioners who are champions and advocates for reaching out to those in need, and who are known for getting things done (either in the parish or in their professional lives), are enough to put together a plan for using new media to catalyze the parish's outreach.

I believe that the best way for the parish to animate parishioners to become agents of the New Evangelization is to establish a new commission. Let me speak, however, to some of the other theoretical options regarding who should, and should not, do this work.

THEORETICAL OPTIONS FOR LEADING THE PARISH'S NEW MEDIA INITIATIVES

- **The pastor or one of the priests on staff:** Because of priests' many pastoral duties, it would be difficult, from a time-management perspective, for them to lead this charge. Also, their taking the lead on this initiative might convey the idea that it is only the priest's job, not the lay faithful's job, to evangelize. It is best that the pastor and priests serve as sponsors and encouragers, not as the project leaders, of this initiative.

- **A member of the parish staff:** Perhaps your parish has someone in charge of outreach to young adults or teens, or someone in charge of adult faith formation or evangelization, or someone who already manages your communications — like bulletins, websites, or social media posts. Nativity Catholic Church in Brandon, Florida, has an electronic outreach director.[29] If so, this person (or another staff member) should be on the initiative team. It is good, however, that this person is not the initiative leader, because a paid staff member leading the effort might create the sense that evangelization and outreach are really the duties of those paid to do it, not every parishioner's duties by virtue of his or her baptism.

- **A parishioner who will volunteer to lead this initiative:** An enthusiastic parishioner with good leadership skills is the best person to take charge of this initiative because it communicates that outreach is an activity of all committed Catholics. However, because a goal is to get all parishioners to see themselves as agents of the New Evangelization, and to reach and involve all parishioners in this initiative, it is more practical to have a team of people to do this — one involving champions who have strong relationships in each of the various demographic segments of the parish. One person is probably still needed to chair the initiative, so it is important to identify someone who can be an effective chair, but to make sure the chair has plenty of help.

- **Part of existing parish committees, such as the parish's pastoral council or evangelization committee:** There is often a fear about establishing new committees because of the expectation that key parish staff leaders, including the pastor, need to attend more meetings. There might be a desire to add a key task to an existing committee or council. However, because any existing committee has a pre-established scope and many other duties, it most likely will not be effective at taking on another major task. Also, practically speaking, many existing parish committees are not "action and initiative" committees but more advisory bodies. Establishing a new commission, therefore, is typically best. There may be some people on existing committees that you could ask to serve on a new commission in addition to (or instead of) their current duties.

WHY ESTABLISHING A NEW COMMISSION IS THE BEST OPTION

You want a lot of help and want to get new people involved. You want to establish a clear, compelling, and motivating mandate. A new commission is a sign that a new era in the parish is beginning. It signals that outreach is such an important priority that you are forming a high-profile commission with a laser-focused purpose to lead the parish into a new era in its communication — all in a way that parishioners can have fun and grow as disciples.

It is also important to believe that to achieve different results we often need a different design. If your evangelization and outreach activities need to be dramatically expanded, you likely need a new structure, system, and process. Starting something new enables innovation and creativity. It also requires a new plan, not simply good intentions, since hope is never a strategy.

What should the commission be called? I recommend **"New Media Outreach Commission."** The word "new" is always good to get people to pay attention. "New Media" communicates what people will be using, but it may require a little education on what new media actually involves. "Outreach" is important because it clearly states that the primary outcome is not to increase communication among parish insiders or increase engagement within the current parish membership. On the contrary, its purpose is to grow the size and influence of the parish community, at least by its social media, among those who are effectively outside the current parish community. "Commission" is better than "Committee" because it includes the word "mission," like Jesus' Great Commission (Mt 28:16-20), and is less familiar than "Committee" (which can often have negative and boring connotations).

What should the initiative be called? I suggest "New Media Outreach Initiative." It is straightforward. Perhaps you may be thinking it is a little boring, but people will understand what it is and what it means. I think it is also helpful that the connection is obvious: the "New Media Outreach Commission" is leading the "New Media Outreach Initiative." This connection between the names provides clarity for everyone.

How many people should be on the commission? In most parishes, I would suggest seven or eight parishioners, along with someone from the parish staff and someone from the parish pastoral council as participating members.

AN EXAMPLE OF A CHARTER FOR THE NEW MEDIA OUTREACH COMMISSION

A charter aligns all members of a commission on the purpose, the goals, the activities, and the way with which the commission will go about its work. It is great when a commission has a simple and clear one-page charter that can quickly be reviewed at each meeting, in a way that inspires and focuses the work of the commission.

There are four main aspects to a successful charter: (1) the commission's charge, (2) the authority and responsibilities of the commission, (3) the composition of the commission, and (4) the norms by which the commission will operate.

There are many good ways to accomplish this, but there is an example charter for a New Media Outreach Commission on pages 74-75. A customizable version of this charter is available on Parish-GuideToNewMedia.com.

RECRUITING THE NEW MEDIA OUTREACH COMMISSION

There are many ways to recruit people to participate on teams and committees. Every leader has personal preferences and techniques that might be adjusted for the type of organization, environment, or challenge.

Some parishes struggle with getting parishioners involved, so I would like to share a possible process for recruiting the commission. The critical steps are identifying the strongest possible candidates and inviting them personally, instead of relying on broadcast announcements at Mass and in the bulletin. There are many parishioners who have never (or rarely) been involved actively in parish ministries because they have never been invited individually, positively, and prayerfully. Their involvement would be a huge gift to the

(Continued on page 76)

73

HOLY APOSTLES PARISH
CHARTER — NEW MEDIA OUTREACH COMMISSION

Jesus said that he came to earth "to seek and to save the lost" (Lk 19:10). Every single person matters to God. And right before he left, Jesus said: "As the Father has sent me, even so I send you" (Jn 20:21). Every single person in our community matters to us. There is nothing in life with a greater purpose than being God's agent to lead people to eternal life and love.

Purpose

The New Media Outreach Commission (NMOC) seeks to help every adult parishioner in our parish embrace new media tools to nurture existing and new relationships within our community, to receive inspirational and formational messages from Holy Apostles Parish, and to tithe 10 percent of his or her own new media messages to help others become or grow as disciples.

Responsibilities of Commission Members

- Commit to being a champion and passionate advocate for the New Media Outreach Initiative because of the impact it will have on everyone the Initiative reaches.

- Assist parish staff to establish Holy Apostles Parish as an effective hub of new media communications — ensuring that it has a great website, social media, and other interactive media tools — which they will be proud to recommend to their friends, to visit and connect with.

Commission Duties

- Form a pilot program of 50 to 100 adult parishioners to participate in a season of technical trainings on new media technology, relationship building online, and outreach. Participate in this pilot phase. Learn from what works and what needs improvement for implementation in the entire parish.

- Create a compelling series of presentation materials that will engage parishioners and get them excited to participate in the New Media Outreach Initiative. Help each parishioner understand and express what the initiative involves.

- Establish a way for parishioners to sign up and commit to participation. Continually and warmly invite those who have not signed up to do so.

- Lead a parish-wide effort to train parishioners on the various new media tools (how to sign up and how to connect with the parish, with other Catholic organizations, and with friends, family members, and neighbors).

- Invite every adult parishioner to report on his or her progress and to become involved in the training and outreach.

- Make the process fun — one that strengthens the bonds of community and friendship in Holy Apostles Parish.

- Monitor progress toward all objectives. Provide progress reports to the parish through the bulletin and parish blog.

Commission Composition

- The Commission will have a chair, a vice-chair, and up to eight other members, representing a diversity of ages, languages, Masses normally attended, and ministry involvement. A good mix of talented media and technical people and those hungry to learn and get others involved should be maintained.

- A member of the Parish Pastoral Council and a member of the parish staff should be included.

- Commission members should have six-month renewable terms.

Commission Operations

- The Commission will communicate weekly through media tools and meet in person at least once a month.

- The Commission will sponsor and offer trainings within the pilot phase and within the general phase weekly for a period of 10 to 12 weeks.

- Minutes from the Commission meetings will be posted on the parish blog (or website).

(Continued from page 73)
parish and could be a huge gift to themselves, as it could change the trajectory of their lives and the lives of others.

A PROCESS FOR INVITING A COMMISSION

1. **Ask Jesus' help.** Pray for God's guidance in discerning which individuals to invite to take on ministry leadership. Reflect on all those with talents already in your parish.

2. **Develop a list of potential commission members.** I recommend that you break this down into several steps. First, gather a list of registered parishioners and a list of everyone who currently leads parish ministries. Then, because not everyone is always registered or currently involved, after each weekend Mass one Sunday, write down people you see there who might be good for the commission. Then identify 25 people that you might want to approach. Do not edit the list at this point; just put about 25 names on it. From this list, select the six to eight candidates who (in your opinion) will contribute most to the commission.

3. **Commit to inviting people individually.** One of the main reasons that people do not get involved in the parish is, "Nobody ever asked me." In this regard, they mean personally and individually, not general messages at the end of Mass or requests in the bulletin.

4. **Share the New Media Outreach Initiative vision with each candidate.** Explain the initiative and review the draft charter for the commission. At this point, clarify that you are only asking them for a six-month commitment to help get the initiative under way.

5. **Offer an initial new media training session for the commission and parish staff.** This training session will ideally be led by someone on the commission or, secondly, from someone at the diocesan office. At the conclusion of this training session, officially commission the group as they begin their work.

6. **Begin regular meetings.**

SUMMARY POINTS

- A team (commission) provides the human resources necessary to carry out a large initiative and to reach the entire parish. A newly formed commission signals that this is a significant priority and the beginning of a new effort. It also allows for creativity and innovation, as well as the opportunity to involve new leaders within the parish.

- Select an initiative and commission name that is straightforward (and easy to remember) so that everyone naturally understands what its work is about and that is easy to remember.

- Develop a simple one-page charter that defines the work and motivates people to want to engage in the commission's transformative work.

- The forming of a commission is a prayerful, deliberate, and intentional process. Start by recruiting possible chairs, then recruiting key leaders, and then rounding out the commission membership to allow it to reach the entire parish effectively.

REFLECTION AND DISCUSSION QUESTIONS

What have been the best committee experiences you have ever had (at work and at the parish)? What made them great experiences?

•••

How might you improve and customize the draft charter above for your own parish situation?

•••

Why have you become involved in volunteer activities within your parish, the Church, or in other organizations? What can be learned from those experiences to help invite and recruit new Church ministers/volunteers?

•••

Why do you think an individual invitation is more effective than a general broadcasted invitation (through pulpit or bulletin announcement) in recruiting Church-ministries and commission members?

Chapter Six

A CONSISTENT DIGITAL IDENTITY

"It is not enough to be passersby on the digital highways, simply 'connected'; connections need to grow into true encounters. We cannot live apart, closed in on ourselves. We need to love and to be loved. We need tenderness."[30]

POPE FRANCIS, MESSAGE FOR THE 48TH WORLD COMMUNICATIONS DAY, JANUARY 24, 2014

One of the first steps for a parish to consider when committing to a strong new media outreach effort is to intentionally pick a digital identity that is easy to deploy across various methods (websites, blogs, Facebook, Twitter, Google+, YouTube, Vimeo, and so on).

A Catholic-parish example of the application of a consistent digital identity is the Church of the Nativity in Timonium, Maryland, which we discussed in Chapter One. The staff there focused the parish's digital identity on "ChurchNativity." Much of their related websites and digital identities start with "Nativity":

- **Parish website:** ChurchNativity.tv (pastor's blog: NativityPastor .tv)

- **Twitter:** @ChurchNativity (or Twitter.com/ChurchNativity)

- **Facebook:** facebook.com/ChurchNativity

- **Videos:** Linked off their website

- **Live webcasts:** live.ChurchNativity.tv

- **Pinterest:** Pinterest.com/ChurchNativity

Elements of a Strong Digital Identity

The goal of a consistent digital identity is to make it easy for people (those you are trying to reach in order to deepen their faith) to find you.

A consistent digital identity involves many elements.

Name

Your parish's digital identity should be intuitive. Consider what newcomers might type into a search engine if they were looking for a Catholic church in your area. That will likely be a better name for growth and evangelization than something only active parishioners might know. Since abbreviations also are things that only insiders and active parishioners might know, I recommend that you spell out full names, even if it makes your digital identity a bit longer. A goal is to have a name that is easy to say and remember (one that parishioners or seekers effortlessly can repeat to others).

In choosing a name, there are two approaches to consider. One approach is to start by considering the name of your parish, putting it with your town, and then adding dot-org (.org), if it is available, to the end (for example, SaintABCTownname.org). This dot-org domain extension was specifically created for non-profit organizations. Dot-Catholic (.Catholic) will be available at some time in the next several years for Catholic parishes and, at that point, would be my recommended extension. For now, if dot-org is not available, look for dot-net (.net) or one of the various other extensions available from one of the domain registration services, such as Register.com. If dot-com (.com) and dot-net are also available, I recommend that you buy those too and have them pointed (automatically forwarded) to your dot-org website, to ensure that someone else does not purchase these to confuse your parishioners.

PURCHASING A DOMAIN NAME

If your parish chooses to work with a company to develop and enhance your website, the company often will help the parish register the website. It is important that the parish clearly own the domain in this process, in case an issue arises with the company or individual that registered the domain.

There are many Internet services that provide domain registration and website hosting, such as NameCheap.com, Name.com, BlueHost.com and Register.com. Generally, it costs about $10 a year to secure and renew a domain. Every hosting provider has slightly different terms for how much it costs to host a domain. If you are working with a Catholic web-development firm, it will often host the website as part of its fee.

A list of Catholic web-development firms and a longer list of domain registrars and helpful links are available on ParishGuideTo NewMedia.com.

St. Joseph Parish in Holbrook, Massachusetts, chose this route to select StJosephHolbrook.org as their website name and digital identity. In doing so, it elected to utilize the "St." abbreviation for "Saint." The advantages of this choice are that it is shorter and that most Catholics understand the abbreviation. The downside is that you often may need to spell it out for clarity. The other approach is to use the full five letters, like SaintBernadetteFallRiver.com, and then after saying the name, state that it is all spelled out. My preference is to spell everything out, because I believe it is easier for people to remember.

The other general approach with names is to combine your town and the word Catholic, particularly if there is only one parish in town or if all the parishes work in a collaborative way, with one team (i.e., TownnameCatholic.org). For example, in Lexington, Massachusetts, the two parishes of St. Brigid and Sacred Heart share a pastor and chose to adopt the digital identity of LexingtonCatholic.org.

I think it is generally good to add "Catholic" to the name, despite making it longer, because it reinforces our tradition and identity, as well as likely making it easier for newcomers to find you if they search "Catholic" and your town name on Google and other search engines.

It is important also to ensure that the domain name is registered and owned by the parish, not an employee or a volunteer. There have been some issues in the Archdiocese of Boston where a well-intentioned parishioner establishes an online presence and then moves away — in some cases, the parish hasn't been able to get the domain transferred to itself, so the parish needed to establish an entirely new website.

A Central Platform ("Mothership")

To simplify a parish's activities on the digital continent, it is helpful to have one central platform to which all of its social media relate. As we discussed in Chapter Two, the Pontifical Council for Social Communications established News.va as the "mothership" for all the news associated with Pope Francis and the Vatican. Facebook posts, news articles, and other media are linked to it.

For most parishes, the best platform will be the parish website with a built-in blog. This can be optimized and laid out in a way that will encourage parishioners to return there each day for materials to grow in faith, to link to various posts, and to check the parish calendar. We will discuss this much more in the next two chapters.

Logo or Picture

Pick a consistent photo that can be used in all new media platforms. Most of the time it can be a professionally taken photo of the Church or a distinctive element of the church, like a steeple. In other cases, it can be a modern illustration done in a graphics program. Pick one and use it across all the new media elements. Immaculate Heart of Mary Parish in Cincinnati (ihom.org) uses the parish's logo that is an illustration of a heart with a cross inside, with light emanating like a candle at the top and beams of light radiating from it. St. Elizabeth

Ann Seton Parish in Fort Wayne, Indiana (seasfw.org), uses a combination of the parish's logo and a photo of the parish in all its media.

Short Description

Include a short description of the parish that is inviting to all parishioners and possible newcomers.

Holy Name of Jesus Parish in Wayzata, Minnesota, says this: "Holy Name of Jesus is an active, Christ-centered parish located in Wayzata, Minnesota. With a strong focus on hospitality, good liturgy, education, and outreach, our community is one where we hope you feel welcome and a part of our mission."

Our Lady of Good Counsel Parish in Plymouth, Michigan, describes itself this way: "Our Lady of Good Counsel Parish is a Roman Catholic faith community leading people to God the Father through the knowledge and love of Jesus Christ and the guidance of the Holy Spirit."

Background Photos

With some new media tools, such as Twitter and Facebook, there is the opportunity to have background and secondary photos. Photos of the sanctuary or of a fun gathering of the parish might be good here. These images can be changed to reflect colors of the liturgical seasons, to display banners you have in church, to show various photos of elements inside your church that you want to draw attention to, or to be consistent with an increased offertory campaign or parish capital campaign.

Colors, Fonts, and Style

Develop a style guide (i.e., a master document) of colors and fonts, and use those elements consistently across all your media in the digital world.

Catholic Identity

Clearly communicate you are Catholic in a way that shares your joy in your Catholic identity, encouraging spirit and rootedness in our one, holy, apostolic and Catholic faith. Some parishes do this in their website header by identifying as "A Roman Catholic parish of the Diocese of [Name]."

What If You Have Different Names and Inconsistent Identities Now?

After you have picked a new name that is friendly to newcomers, have your website firm (or staff member) point or forward the old website addresses to the new domain address so that people who have bookmarked the old name will automatically go to the new website.

If the old name is on Facebook or Twitter, work with your New Media Outreach Commission to establish the new profile, and then encourage all those connected with the former account to follow or "like" the new account.

What If Your Parish Is Part of a Cluster or a Collaborative of Parishes?

There may be pastoral reasons why the pastor of the cluster or collaborative would want to maintain individual websites, at least for a while, to honor the individual parish communities, cultures, and histories that have developed over time. If this is the approach that is chosen, I would recommend adding a simple website for the collaborative, with a new digital identity, following the principles above. In the short term, the new website could be simply done and include prominent links to each of the respective parishes in the collaborative. An example of this is BeverlyCatholic.com.

I recommend that all the social media accounts be at the cluster or collaborative level, even if there are specific websites for each of the parishes in a collaborative. The digital identity for the social media accounts should match the new identity of the collaborative website.

What If You Are Not Ready Yet to Implement All of the New Media Approaches?

It is important that you register for all the services (Facebook, Twitter, YouTube, Pinterest, Vimeo, Livestream, and so on) with your consistent digital name so that you confirm they are all available and ensure that no other organization or individual registers them first.

SUMMARY POINTS

- Consistency in your name across various new media makes your parish easier to find and easier for your message to get through the clutter of a noisy world.

- Select a name that will be intuitive and easy to find for your target audience (newcomers) and easy to remember for all in your parish community. A combination of parish name and town (e.g., SaintBernadetteFallRiver.com) or a combination of town name and Catholic (e.g., LexingtonCatholic.org) are two recommended approaches.

- Set up the same elements — such as logos, secondary photos, descriptions, fonts, and colors — across all your digital media.

- Even if you are not ready to establish all of the media now, register the names so that you can use them later.

REFLECTION AND DISCUSSION QUESTIONS

Why do you think choosing a name that works well for newcomers will make your outreach through new media more effective? Do you think it is better for newcomers if you spell out or abbreviate the word "saint'" in the digital identity?

•••

Which of the two approaches to selecting a digital domain name do you think is best for newcomers: (1) including the parish name and town (i.e., StJosephHolbrook.org) or (2) including the town name and Catholic (i.e., LexingtonCatholic.org)?

Chapter Seven

A WEBSITE: THE PARISH'S VIRTUAL FRONT DOOR

"We are called to show that the Church is the home of all. Are we capable of communicating the image of such a Church? Communication is a means of expressing the missionary vocation of the entire Church; today the social networks are one way to experience this call to discover the beauty of faith, the beauty of encountering Christ. In the area of communications too, we need a Church capable of bringing warmth and of stirring hearts."[31]

POPE FRANCIS, MESSAGE FOR THE 48TH WORLD
COMMUNICATIONS DAY, JANUARY 24, 2014

In chapter seven of Brandon Vogt's 2011 book, *The Church and New Media*, I wrote that a parish website is a "virtual front door" to the Church and that we want it to be "welcoming, well cared for, and worthy of someone's visit. For example, if a parish church had a dilapidated front door with graffiti on it and a broken sign with outdated Mass times, many that might otherwise want to stop in for a visit might keep on moving. Similarly, New Media vehicles that are out-of-date, out-of-style, and don't warmly welcome newcomers and encourage them to become regular visitors miss a big opportunity."[32]

As a virtual front door to both the parish and the Church, we hope that once seekers and newcomers visit, they will be able to learn much more about what it means to be Catholic. Many parishes will choose to address this simply by providing links to the *Catechism of the Catholic Church*, to papal documents, to diocesan or national Catholic publications, to Catholic media, and to apologetics sites like CatholicAnswers.com. Other options that parishes choose involve signing up for a content service that automatically provides updates several times per week, such as Our Sunday Visitor's "Faith in Action" series for parish websites or by developing content themselves.

A Digital Platform

In addition to being the digital front door to the parish, websites are also the best platform for a parish to house its new media content in an organized way. In treating the website as a platform, the parish will want to draw parishioners to it at least a few times a week and in many cases drive traffic toward it by utilizing social media to encourage people to see a blog post, an article, or a video directly on the parish website. Once they are there, parishioners can explore more of the website's resources and information.

There are many tactics that will motivate parishioners to visit the website regularly throughout the week:

- Provide links on the parish's email, Twitter, and Facebook to articles on the website.

- The CatholicTVjr widget[33] allows people to watch videos of a daily Mass broadcast, videos of the Rosary, and many other programs right on the parish's website.

- A Mass-readings widget[34] encourages Catholics without a *Magnificat* or *Word Among Us* publication to peruse the readings prior to Mass.

- A well-promoted regular schedule of blog posts could become "appointment" visiting. An example blog entry such as "Wednesday Pastor's Post" would bring parishioners there mid-week to connect with resources. Another idea is to have a parish staff member post links to the "Top 3 Catholic News Articles" from either the past week or even past day, which would give people a chance to deepen the connection to the parish, as it forms and engages them in the current events in the life of the Church. These article links could be to diocesan publications or links to Catholic News Service, Catholic News Agency, Our Sunday Visitor, National Catholic Register, Zenit, or Vatican websites such as News.va. Moreover, a series of faith-related questions and answers, with links to apologetical sites, would help parishioners integrate faith and reason and give them tools to discuss the faith in an increasingly secular world.

As a platform, the parish website becomes the digital home base. Parishioners can trust that all important information will be there, in some way, even if information also appears on the parish's social media, such as Facebook and Twitter. If parishioners only visit one place, the website, they will be in the loop.

Holy Name of Jesus Parish in Wayzata, Minnesota, is a good example of a parish that uses its website (hnoj.org) as a digital platform. Clear and easy to find on its website are links to its parish blog, Facebook, and Twitter presences, as well as links to the latest news and events.

What Makes an Effective Parish Website?

Soon after our Catholic Media Secretariat was formed in the Archdiocese of Boston, we determined that one of our key initiatives would be to help our parishes improve their presence on the web.

Our first step was to enlist the help of a graduate intern to review the websites of all 291 parishes. Her initial research concluded that only 31 percent of archdiocesan parishes had a great or good website, 34 percent had an "okay" website (i.e., information was current, but appearance, content, and functionality were very basic), 24 percent had a "lousy" website (information was not current, and appearance, content, and functionality did not present a good image of the Church), and 11 percent of our parishes didn't have a website presence at all in 2011.

Then we wanted to provide a detailed audit of each website, with some recommendations, so she conducted a second round of research. She reviewed all the publications available at the time about which elements make for a good parish or ministry website, compiled a list of attributes, and then evaluated each parish on these dimensions.

We segmented all the characteristics into three areas: (1) appearance and navigation (how easy it is to find the information visitors are looking for on the site); (2) content and information; and (3) user-friendly functionality (and technical elements). In our parish website training sessions, we noted that appearance and navigation can go from "current" to "dated" quickly, but that content and user-friendly functionality are longer-lasting. (Please see Appendix III — "Rate Your Parish Website Tool" — for a list of the 72 website attributes we evaluated.)

> ### LEADING THE WAY: INSIGHTS FROM LISA TAYLOR AND SEAN ATER OF IMMACULATE HEART OF MARY PARISH IN CINCINNATI (IHOM.ORG)

Question: What do you believe are the most important elements of a great parish website today?

Lisa Taylor and Sean Ater: We developed an acronym, P.R.A.I.S.E., when building our webpage, that identified the most important elements of a successful webpage:

P

- *Purpose:* Why do you have a website? Does your website support the overall mission, vision, and goals of your parish?

- *Parish:* What is "unique" about your parish? (Unique selling proposition.)

- *People:* How are *you* going to help *them*? Are you answering their questions? Are you reaching outward into the community?

- *Photos:* Do you have high-quality photos to represent the culture of your parish?

- *Pastor:* Could your pastor write a dynamic weekly blog or monthly topical message?

R

- *Reaction:* What do you want visitors to do when they get to your site? Explore? Join? Give? Is your site user-friendly and simple to browse?

- *Religious:* How are you representing the beauty of our Catholic religion?

- *Relationships:* How are you building relationships? Online? Offline? In the parish? In the community?

- *Results:* How are you tracking your results?

A

- *Audience:* Who is your target audience? (Marketing to everyone is marketing to no one.)

- *Awareness:* Who is being served in your community by your parish? Are you meeting the needs of your parishioners with your website?

- *Action:* What is the "call to action"? Are you asking anything of the visitor to your website?

I

- *Inviting:* Is your homepage inviting to look at? Does it invite the visitor to explore further? Is your body copy well written? Is the "tone" consistent throughout the pages?

- *Information:* Do you have all the "basic" information on your website, such as Mass times, parish address, phone number, and directions?

- *Inspiration:* Do you include inspiring stories about your parishioners in either written or digital form? (Make your message memorable by placing it into a story.)

S

- *Social Media:* Is your site taking advantage of the latest in social media?

- *S.E.O. — Search Engine Optimization:* Are you taking full advantage of Search Engine Optimization? Are people finding your site? Once they find your site, are they staying?

- *Search:* Does your website have a "search" feature and a site map?

E

- *Evangelization:* Is your site mission driven or member driven? Are you using your site to evangelize the seeker and the disengaged?

- *Engaging:* Is your site engaging? Is your site cluttered or is the content focused? Will users be encouraged to make repeated visits?

- *Events:* Are your events featured on your homepage? Do your events answer the *Who, What, When, Where,* and *Why?*

    See ParishGuideToNewMedia.com for additional insights from IHOM.org and other award-winning parish websites.

One of the new technologies available for parish websites is the ability to live stream (webcast) liturgies and seminars. Church of the Nativity Parish in Maryland has branded this an "online campus," as it has allowed travelers to connect with the parish liturgies while they are on the road and to allow seekers to experience what liturgies there are like if they are discerning whether to visit the parish in person. Nativity uses a service called ChurchOnlinePlatform.com. St. Monica's Parish in Santa Monica, California, utilizes Livestream.com for the webcasts of their Sunday liturgies.[35]

Here are a few best practices that experienced parishes recommend:

- Include a prominent menu item or graphic for "newcomers" to make your website welcoming to those discerning whether to become part of your parish community.

- With electronic registration forms, make sure that private data is not collected. If you take payments, ensure that this is done through a service that meets the security standards in place today.

- Adopt policies on using photos from parish events on your website. Some parents will not want photos of their children online. Individuals may request to have a photo removed because they do not want themselves online or they do not like the photo. These requests should all be satisfied without hesitation. (Please see Appendix VII for examples of social media norms for additional guidance on pictures with children.)

- Be careful about copying and pasting web content onto your own website (even with the proper attributions) without gaining permission or licensing it for the parish. When in doubt, it is better to have a direct link to the content (where you originally discovered it) than to copy and paste it onto your own website.

- If the parish's website has multiple content managers and contributors, write down the workflow for reviewing and approving content, and determine when content managers can post to the site without approval.

- Measure your progress of increasing the number of visitors to your website and each of the content areas by using free analytical tools, such as Google Analytics. In this way, you can see which pages are visited most often and ensure those areas of the site are accurate and up-to-date.

- Host your website with a web-hosting service like Blue Host instead of a dedicated server.

Our Archdiocesan Efforts to Improve the Online Website Presence of Our Parishes

After we presented our website findings to parishes and shared with them their individual website assessments, our new media office received many requests for direct assistance to implement our recommended best practices. We helped 10 parishes directly and then determined that we were unable to keep up with the demand — a good problem to have!

We concluded that the best way to scale (grow) our ability to help all archdiocesan parishes would be to partner with a website firm that concentrated on parishes, and one that was large enough that we felt confident it would continue to be in ministry. (Many website providers only have one to three professionals, and we considered this risky if one of the principals exited the organization for any reason.)

Our team had worked closely with Our Sunday Visitor's Offertory Solutions division (osvoffertory.com) on reviewing and sharing their Online Giving product with archdiocesan parishes. Parishes had appreciated that OSV had been started by a Catholic priest over a century ago, remained a nonprofit organization that shared operating surpluses with the Church through the OSV Institute, and maintained strong customer service. When OSV indicated that it was planning to offer website solutions for parishes in late 2011, we were enthusiastic to work with the company, as we knew from experience that OSV would be a good partner for our parishes and our diocesan new media team.

Our Sunday Visitor's website development team utilized the website research we had done to develop templates for archdiocesan parishes. They have further developed these templates and added many others that integrate OSV's publishing content in the time since.

For a reasonable setup fee and one monthly fee for support, hosting, and service, parishes are able to maintain websites that have current technology, that work in various formats, and that represent among the best and latest website technology in the country.

LEADING THE WAY: INSIGHTS FROM JOE LUEDTKE OF CATHOLICTECHTALK.COM

Question: What are the elements of a good parish website?

Joe Luedtke: To have a *good* website, you need to deliver two basic needs for the parishioner or general visitor to your site. These should be easy to meet but are often overlooked in the quest to build a great website:

Updated content: This requires a website that is simple, ridiculously simple to maintain. Your church secretary or priest needs to be able to update the site. No programming experience should be necessary. You should have more than one person updating your site and be doing so weekly. You need to select a website solution that facilitates this.

Critical content: Eighty percent of all church website traffic is searching for one of these three items:

- **Mass times:** Your current mass schedule with upcoming holy days.

- **Event calendar:** This week, this month's, and next month's events within your church.

- **Your church bulletin:** The bulletin is still the staple of church communication. Even though *all* of the bulletin content *should* be on the church website, it's typically not, and a large percentage of your website visitors want to just download your church bulletin.

Question: What differentiates great from good parish websites?

Luedtke: I think it's engagement. If you would randomly look at 10 parish websites around the country, what would they most have in common? Chances are that one thing that would stand out is that most of them would have a picture of their building on the homepage. Sure, there are some beautiful churches out there, but there's more to our faith than our buildings! Where are the people? The cross? Other symbols of our faith?

I'm hoping we see less architectural photos of church buildings and more examples, both in imagery and content, that show a vibrant faith community. Does your website demonstrate engagement? Can parishioners sign up for an email newsletter on your website? Whether it's through photos or a Facebook or Twitter feed, how can your website illustrate that you have indeed a vibrant and active church community?

People want to belong to a group of like-minded individuals and feel welcome by their priest, parish staff, and their entire parish community. That's the community we need to build within the Church and online.

See ParishGuideToNewMedia.com for additional insights from Joe Luedtke.

EXAMPLES OF EFFECTIVE PARISH WEBSITES

Many parishes in the Archdiocese of Boston embraced our approach and selected an Our Sunday Visitor website template for their parish. Four examples are:

- Sacred Heart Parish in Quincy, Massachusetts (SacredHeartQuincy.org)

- Holy Family Parish in Duxbury, Massachusetts (HolyFamilyDuxbury.org)

- St. Margaret Parish in Burlington, Massachusetts (StMargaretBurlington.org)

- St. Mary of the Annunciation Parish in Danvers, Massachusetts (StMaryDanvers.org)

I encourage you to visit these websites. Each utilizes a similar template, but they've personalized the content and the structure for their communities.

Nationally, CatholicTechTalk.com began a parish website contest in 2012.[36] Joe Luedtke and the other Catholic technology enthusiasts behind the website started the contest to raise awareness, and hopefully to help parishes raise the bar. Joe commented: "We created our Parish Website of the Year contest to recognize those churches that have truly created exceptional websites, but more importantly to give others a model to follow and examples to review. Our evaluation criteria and winners should provide a good framework and examples to follow. Winning is always a nice feather in one's cap, but it's really meant to be about sharing and spreading the good (technical) word!" (Please see the sidebar on page 94 for other insights from Joe Luedtke on what makes a good website and what he sees as important current website issues.)

In 2013, CatholicTechTalk.com recognized the following parishes for their websites:

- Immaculate Heart of Mary Parish in Cincinnati, Ohio (IHOM. org)

- St. Thomas More Parish in Sarasota, Florida (StThomasMoresrq. org)

- St. Gabriel the Archangel Parish in St. Gabriel, Louisiana (StGabrielCatholicChurch.com)

Each of the websites has strengths that parishes across the United States and the world can seek to emulate. To appreciate a website, you need to view it, so please visit ParishGuideToNewMedia.com to see screenshots, evaluations, and links for each of the above websites.

INSIGHTS FROM CHAD BABIN OF ST. GABRIEL THE ARCHANGEL PARISH IN ST. GABRIEL, LOUISIANA (STGABRIELCATHOLICCHURCH.COM)

Chad Babin: The first impression we hope to create with St. Gabriel's website is a feeling of invitation. I like to see visitors taken in by artistic imagery of the church and parish grounds, making it a real place of community and worship. My goal is that people will say to themselves, "I want to visit this parish!"

The most important elements of a great parish website are timely, community-driven content and a design that best reflects what makes your church-parish unique. Visitors need to see your website as an accurate and timely source for parish news and events. Also, our parish of St. Gabriel has a long, 240-year history. I feel it is important to reflect that rich history in the design and layout of the parish website. It is a great aspect which sets our parish website apart and makes it special.

The role of a church website in parish communications and evangelization is not just to inform but also to encourage parishioners and newcomers to participate and attend campus events and Masses. Church happens when members congregate. In our parish, we strive to build family and community. Encouraging website visitors to attend functions and liturgies should be a goal in communicating and evangelizing, which furthers the communal life of the church.

Website elements that are most important to parishioners are the ability to stay informed about upcoming events and to easily sign up online for parish ministries. You can never give someone too many opportunities to contact the parish or to get involved. For newcomers, Mass times and contact information are essential and should be on the homepage. Another important element, especially for newcomers, is to incorporate pictures of your church into your website. I'm surprised at how many church websites I visit which have no imagery of their church or grounds. I believe newcomers will be more open to visiting your parish if they know what is offered there visually and ministerially.

Having video presentations produced in the parish on our website has created a dynamic that has really engaged our visitors. Videos have the ability to catch one's attention and have given the parish a unique avenue for teaching and evangelization. By having new videos for parish campaigns, different liturgical seasons, and messages from our pastor on St. Gabriel's website, it has encouraged members of the congregation to become more involved in ministries and Mass celebrations.

See ParishGuideToNewMedia.com for additional insights from St. Gabriel the Archangel Parish.

STEPS TO ENHANCING YOUR PARISH WEBSITE
- Evaluate your parish's website, utilizing the tool provided by CatholicTechTalk.com in Appendix III.

- Review the effective websites listed above and at Parish GuideToNewMedia.com. Determine the elements you like the most from each of the sites, for review with a website designer.

- Work with a website designer to upgrade all the aspects of your website as a digital platform. A great way to find one is to look at the footer of parish websites that you like. The website design firm is often linked there.

- Submit your website for consideration each year in the Catholic Tech Talk contest. Learn from the parishes that are finalists and award winners. Parishes across the country can help one another raise the bar each year through participation in contests like the one at Catholic Tech Talk.

Ken Perry, from St. Aloysius Parish in Jackson, New Jersey (saintaloysiusonline.org), a 2012 CatholicTechTalk.com website award-winning parish, provided this general advice to parishes considering a website upgrade:

> We are planning a redesign ourselves. My advice would be not doing it alone. There are plenty of other churches out there — Catholic, Protestant, and Mormon (they do a nice job) — who do an excellent job with their websites. Seek them out! Take a look at what they've done. Look to the evangelical churches, which do a fantastic job communicating on the web. Do a Google search for "great church websites"! Call those churches up, and ask them why they made the decisions they did.

SUMMARY POINTS

- A parish's website is its "virtual front door" and its "digital platform and home base" for all new media activity. It is worth the investment and commitment to keep current. The website is likely the first impression that will be created for newcomers and seekers for both the parish and for the (universal) Church.

- Parishes would be wise to set a goal and select tactics that encourage parishioners to visit the parish website for new content at least a couple of times during the workweek, if not daily.

- There are many aspects and attributes that lead to an effective parish website. There is no need for each parish to "reinvent the wheel" if it partners with a website-solutions provider that focuses on serving Catholic parishes.

- The Church would be strengthened if all parishes were to set a high bar for their digital presence, annually evaluated their efforts against the parishes nominated and selected by parish website contests, and committed to a path of continuous improvement.

REFLECTION AND DISCUSSION QUESTIONS

What do you think is most important for newcomers and seekers to find when they first visit a parish website? What information do you think is most important for regular parishioners to find when they visit the parish homepage?

•••

How would you compare your current parish website against the examples of effective parish websites in this chapter? What is your favorite website of all those listed and why?

Chapter Eight
BLOGS: INTEGRATING COMMUNICATIONS

"Welcome to my new blog, The Gospel In The Digital Age. *I'm very excited about this new way of communicating, and I hope that it will prove to be an effective way for me to not only share what's on my mind, but also to hear back from you. First, let me begin with a bit of a confession. I'm really a rookie at all things related to the computer, so I'm going to be getting help having these posted. However, having read the theme for our Holy Father's next World Communications Day Message,* The Priest and Pastoral Ministry in the Digital Age: New Media at the Service of the Word, *I thought it was time for me to get involved…. Please bear with me as this effort gets underway. My enthusiasm is genuine and I look forward to having the opportunity to be in regular communication with you. God bless! Stay tuned! God is everywhere, even on the blog!"*[37]

CARDINAL TIMOTHY DOLAN, ARCHBISHOP OF NEW YORK, IN HIS FIRST BLOG POST, OCTOBER 9, 2009

The word "blog" comes from the contraction of the words "web" and "log" (as in "logging" your time or activities). Most blogs are discussion or informational sites published on the Internet in separate entries, articles, and posts. Compared to typical websites, blogs are often less formal and more conversational in tone and approach, more dynamic in content, and more interactive, in the form of comments and discussion in response to posts.

As blogging software has evolved, it has become very easy to share and integrate the various types of digital media (e.g., photos, videos, audio, text, and links) all in one post in a way that can tell a compelling story. I loved blogging from Rome during the 2013 conclave on TheGoodCatholicLife.com about the experiences of being a "pilgrim from Boston" during the important transition of the papacy. Blogging allows bloggers to vividly tell a story by integrating all these digital media.

For example, my post on March 13, 2013, entitled "What it was like to be in St. Peter's Square when Pope Francis was elected," included 2,700 words, three private video messages from my iPhone uploaded to YouTube, three external video links, three audio recordings of the reaction of the crowd, and 25 of George Martell's photos. Through all of these formats, I was able to recount the emotions, experiences, sights, and sounds of seeing the white smoke, hearing the name of Cardinal Bergoglio, and then witnessing the profound gestures and words of our new Pope Francis. The feedback from our audience was that they "felt like they were there in the square." It strikingly demonstrated to me the power of blogging as a communication tool, not only for a diocesan communications ministry but also for our parishes.[38]

A parish blog would be a great place for the New Media Outreach Commission to share information that updates parishioners and motivates them to become involved. Any briefings could be posted there, and videotaped trainings or tutorials could be shared.

KEY REASONS FOR PARISHES TO INCLUDE BLOGS ON THEIR WEBSITES
- **Blogs allow a parish to focus its online efforts, drive traffic to it, and ultimately serve as the nexus of its social network.** Once readers are there on the website, they can be exposed to

the rest of the material on the website in the top menus and other links and graphics on the site. Typical blog posts for a parish would be homilies (text, video, or audio), the pastor's bulletin messages, updates, and images of significant parish events (First Communions, confirmations, funerals, baptisms, speakers, and retreats), and promotions of parish events with links to RSVP.

- **It is easy to share blog posts widely.** Every time a parish posts a blog entry, it can copy the link and send it out by email, Facebook, and Twitter. Or, for a small investment of time, parishes can enable an email management system to share the post with the parish's email list (either as a link or the entire content). Most blogging software systems also allow plug-ins to be installed so that a new blog post is instantly shared with parishioners through the parish's Facebook and Twitter accounts.

- **In most cases, blogs are easier to update and more flexible than a typical website**. Often text from a prepared document can be pasted there, and then images, links, and videos could be inserted and the blog message published.

- **Blogs are particularly a great place to share video and audio recordings with your parish community**. I often write an introduction or a commentary to a video or audio message, and blogs make it easy to keep that introduction together with the video in one focused post. Recordings of Mass homilies can be easily uploaded to the parish blog and shared with all those unable to attend the Mass (or those who want to share the homily they heard at Mass with friends and relatives across the country). If the priest or deacon has a call-to-action at the end of the homily, that call-to-action can be included as text below the video/audio for emphasis. Christ the King Parish in Ann Arbor, Michigan (ctkcc.net), and Our Lady of Good Counsel in Plymouth, Michigan (olgcparish.net), do a strong job of posting audio recordings of homilies and presentations.

- **Blogs can involve parishioners in a digital conversation and foster a good dialogue through the comment function.** When parishioners (or those that parishioners forward the message to) share their reflections after reading the post, the dialogue connects parishioners more deeply with the parish, the pastor, and with one another as they engage in the digital world. In the above example, if the priest or deacon asks a provocative question at the end of his homily, it can be restated at the end of the blog entry, and viewers can respond in the comment section of the blog. (I'll discuss comment policies and best practices later.)

- **A parish with rich and varied content on its website can also utilize its blog to drive traffic to one particular area of its website**. This provides opportunities to focus attention on particular ministry opportunities or faith resources — one at a time — so that parishioners (and all those your parishioners will share the information with) are exposed to all that the parish has to offer digitally.

Practical Advice for Starting a Parish Blog

When the parish decides to start a blog, here are some considerations:

- **Determine if you want to name the blog**. If you do name it, consider a general name that can encompass all of parish life, pastoral activity, and the shared Christian journey. Pick a name that communicates that any parish staff member or ministry leader might post (not just the pastor). Our Lady of Good Counsel Parish in Plymouth, Michigan, chose the name *OLGC Blog* (olgcblog.com). Father Michael White, from Nativity Parish in Timonium, Maryland, chose *Nativity Pastor* for his blog (NativityPastor.tv).

- **Pick a blogging schedule and be consistent**. I recommend blogging at least once per week on a regular day, such as Monday, to summarize the weekend or post a homily, Wednesday to focus parishioners on mid-week spiritual growth, or Friday to promote the weekend events. I think it would be great, however, if parishioners were encouraged to go to the parish website daily (at least Monday-Friday) to receive messages. *OLGC Blog* typically has two to three posts per week, including one that provides the Sunday readings for parishioners to read and reflect on before attending the Sunday Mass.

- **Consider a third-party blogging platform for your blog if your parish website does not have the capabilities to integrate a blog.** If you do so, consider shifting your entire website to a platform that enables blogging, to make it easy to share content. We have been pleased with WordPress for TheGoodCatholicLife. com and other archdiocesan blogs and websites. More information about blogging platforms can be found on Parish GuideToNewMedia.com.

- **Always include images.** After an engaging title and a strong lead paragraph, the next most important element of an attractive and inviting blog post is a good image or embedded video (when a video posted elsewhere is included on your blog page). Photos can be taken from a parish photo library, a screenshot of a good website, or a photo from a service like istockphoto.com or dreamstime.com). CardinalSeansBlog.org is known for the many great images Cardinal Seán O'Malley includes in his weekly posts on Friday evenings.

- **Write in a conversational tone.** Bloggers on the parish website should imagine they are speaking to one person as they write. Of course, if you are posting a homily or bulletin column, the tone might be different. Bloggers may choose, however, to write a conversational introduction to the homily or bulletin column and also to give a conversational conclusion, perhaps by asking a thought-provoking question to get the conversation started in the comment box.

- **Keep things short, engaging, and personal.** Short is always good for regular blog posts so that readers can process the main points quickly and then decide whether to share them with friends in their social network or respond with a reflection in the comment section. Exceptions should be made when you are summarizing an event or pasting a homily. If you have a lot to say about a particular topic, consider segmenting the content into several posts of shorter size that have links to the other entries on the topic. To keep blogs engaging, think about starting many paragraphs with a question that you answer and frame the text for conversation. Write in the first person as much as possible and share personal reflections or comments. People want to know about and trust the messenger as they process the message in the post.

- **Let the blog evolve based on the feedback you receive from your audience.** If you succeed in making the blog interactive and the start of many digital conversations, you will find that some types of posts get shared more than others. You will hear feedback from parishioners that they liked a particular post directly, as well as feedback in the comment boxes. Let that feedback shape future blog posts and expect that the parish blog will evolve and improve over time.

- **See 30 blog-post ideas in Appendix IV.**

Encouraging Blog Comments and Dialogue

Blogs are an effective and efficient way to share information and perspectives digitally, to drive traffic to your website platform, and one of the best ways to begin a great digital conversation. The best blogs have high numbers of comments and shares through social media. How can your parish increase the number of comments and best manage the commenting process?

Here are some practical suggestions for those posting blogs on the parish website:

- **End posts with a question.** Make it clear that you hope that people will share their perspectives too, as you would in an in-person meeting.

- **Be present in the comment section.** Someone from the New Media Outreach Commission should monitor the comments section. There is no need to respond to every comment. Bloggers may want to thank people for their participation and offer clarifications if people misunderstood a post or an aspect of the Catholic faith. You also may want to take conversations "offline" by suggesting to someone who places a sensitive or controversial comment that he or she contact you at the parish office.

- **Publicize a clear comment policy and communicate it often.** This will keep the conversation civil. One important policy decision is whether you will allow anonymous comments.

StrangeNotions.com, a blog for dialogue between Catholics and atheists, has these policies: (1) use your real name; (2 and 3) feel free to disagree ... but understand the position first; (4) critique ideas, not people; (5) engage the argument, not the source; (6) stay on topic; (7) keep it short; (8) help moderate (by letting the blog host know if a comment violates any of the above rules).[39]

- **Be careful to respect copyrights.** Much of the material on the web is copyrighted, including images, blog posts, news articles, and videos. When in doubt, link to someone's quote instead of cutting and pasting it directly onto your site, or ask permission of the blog author to copy and paste it.[40] (See the endnote for some helpful resources on what constitutes fair use of materials on a blog.)

- **Accept that there will be some constructive criticism of your posts or your parish**. This can be tough to see at first, but often such comments offer an opportunity to connect with the critics and lead them to a different place, or to get feedback that can make the parish stronger. People can be moved if you respond civilly and thank them for the suggestion. Receiving constructive criticism effectively is one of the best ways to show that the parish listens and that the blog is a two-way communication forum.

- **Immediately remove the comments by trolls; ban individuals if they become regular trollers.** A troll, in Internet slang, is a person that comments on blogs with the intention to provoke discord or harass the authors, commenters, or community. Their comments can often upset people through their inflammatory or off-topic messages. The best thing to do is to remove their comments immediately. You could then reach out to them by email and remind them of your comment policy. Your blogging software will allow you to delete any inflammatory comment and also to ban people if they become repeat offenders. If your parish is going through a difficult transition and contains several angry commenters, you may choose to enable your system to approve comments before they are posted, although this is more work for someone on your New Media Outreach Commission. I would recommend you only do this if it is necessary and start with open commenting, guided by your comment policy.

MEASURING THE REACH AND EFFECTIVENESS OF YOUR BLOG AND WEBSITE

A good activity for the parish New Media Outreach Commission is to gather statistics on the parish website and blog. An easy and free way to do this is to sign up for a free Google Analytics[41] account, which will give the parish access to a plethora of stats on its blog and website traffic. Sample statistics include: "Unique Visitors" per month, "Page Views" per month, "Percent Change" in the past 12 months, most-popular pages, most-popular referral sources (do they find your site by typing in your website, going through Google, or clicking on a Facebook, Twitter, or email link?), and much more.

If your blog doesn't have comment statistics, consider signing up for a service like Disqus, and track the total number of blog subscribers, the average number of comments per post, and other stats.

After determining the stats you will measure monthly, set goals to increase each key stat every month. If you run out of ideas for how to do that, write a blog post about it and ask your parishioners.

PUBLICIZING YOUR BLOG POSTS

Blogs can be a great tool to attract viewers to your parish website. But what are some of the easiest and most effective ways to draw traffic to your blog posts? We'll discuss that next in Chapter Nine.

SUMMARY POINTS

- Blogs are discussion or informational sites published on the Internet in separate entries, articles, and posts. They are often less formal and more conversational in tone and approach, more dynamic in content, and more interactive in the form of comments and discussion in response to the post. Blogs can be an effective way of beginning a conversation with someone who is lost and away from the Church.

- Parishes can start a blog to focus online efforts, drive traffic to the website, make it easier to share parish information on the website and through social media, integrate video and other forms of media on the website, and encourage reflection and dialogue in the comment section.

- Picking a consistent blogging schedule and sticking to it is important. Ideally, parishes would post a short blog entry once a day. There are many possible topics (30 ideas are listed in Appendix IV).

- Managing the comment discussion is an important part of a robust blog. Bloggers are the stewards of the dialogue in the comment section and should often communicate the comment policy and take simple steps when comments violate those standards.

REFLECTION AND DISCUSSION QUESTIONS

What are five blog topics that members of your parish community would be most interested in reading regularly?

•••

What are your favorite blogs (any subject) and favorite Catholic blogs? Why do you like them?

Chapter Nine

EMAIL, TWITTER, FACEBOOK: SHARING AND DIALOGUE

"The challenge facing social networks is how to be truly inclusive: thus they will benefit from the full participation of believers who desire to share the message of Jesus and the values of human dignity which his teaching promotes. Believers are increasingly aware that, unless the Good News is made known also in the digital world, it may be absent in the experience of many people for whom this existential space is important."[42]

POPE BENEDICT XVI, MESSAGE FOR THE 47TH WORLD COMMUNICATIONS DAY, JANUARY 24, 2013

Parish websites and blogs become the parish's digital home base and platform. Digital pioneer Michael Hyatt says a home base is the place where your most loyal and frequent readers gather and where you direct your online traffic.[43] Monsignor Paul Tighe similarly has referred to News.va as the "mothership" of all Vatican news and information.

How does your parish promote the material on the website (and on the blog) and point parishioners directly there? The simple answer is every way you can, including:

- **Word of mouth:** Mass announcements and pulpit pitches.

- **Printed parish media:** Bulletins, pew cards, handouts, and posters.

- **Email:** Still an effective tool to reach your parishioners.

- **Social media**: Places such as Facebook, Twitter, Google+, LinkedIn, and many other tools. (It seems like new tools get developed every year.)

This chapter will focus on utilizing email and social media like Facebook and Twitter to share parish announcements, website resources, and all new blog posts with those in your parish and with all their digital friends, if your parishioners share the messages. Each of these tools can be used to have a conversation, in which you can hear back from all those who received your messages.

One of the critical duties of a parish's New Media Outreach Commission will be to encourage parishioners to become active at using email, Facebook, Twitter, and other tools to deepen friendships and connect people to what is happening at the parish. The commission can also offer training on best practices for email and various levels of beginning, intermediate, and advanced use of social media tools.

Because email, Facebook, Twitter, and other social tools are free or very inexpensive, the utilization of these methods can be a game changer for parish communications, as it can save printing and postage funds, ensure that messages get received by more people, track feedback on your messages, and much more.

The popular tools may change over time, but their function of efficiently sharing information and beginning a conversation will continue to be an important part of all social media. As Bishop Ronald Herzog has eloquently stated to all of the U.S. bishops, social media is not a fad. We must learn to think, live, and embrace life in a parish with social media. But first, let us start with email.

LEARNING TO THINK, LIVE, AND EMBRACE LIFE ON THE DIGITAL CONTINENT

"The participation in this new form of media is staggering. Media ecologists and other communication experts cite several reasons for the phenomenal growth: a low threshold of investment, both in user knowledge and finances, especially given its reach, the opportunity for immediate dialogue and conversation that transcends geographical and other physical barriers, and the speed in universal adaption....

"Although social media has been around for less than 10 years, it doesn't have the makings of a fad. We're being told that it is causing as fundamental a shift in communication patterns and behavior as the printing press did 500 years ago. And I don't think I have to remind you of what happened when the Catholic Church was slow to adapt to that new technology. By the time we decided to seriously promote that common folk should read the Bible, the Protestant Reformation was well underway....

"It takes careful strategizing and planning to make social media an effective and efficient communication tool, not only for your communications department, but for all of the church's ministries. We digital immigrants need lessons on the digital culture, just as we expect missionaries to learn the cultures of the people they are evangelizing. We have to be enculturated. It's more than just learning how to create a Facebook account. It's learning how to think, live, and embrace life on the Digital Continent."[44]

— Bishop Ronald Herzog of Alexandria, Louisiana, the chairman of the U.S. Bishops' Communications Committee, "Social Media: Friend or Foe, Google or Hornswoggle?," address to the U.S. Conference of Catholic Bishops at their annual meeting, November 15, 2010

EMAIL FOR PARISHES

Email can often be overlooked as a digital communication tool for parishes due to the fact that Facebook and Twitter have done such an effective job of showing their huge impact in the world through their penetration rates. For example, as of this writing, there are more than one billion Facebook accounts worldwide.

Within the United States, the number of households utilizing email is likely still higher than Facebook and Twitter. At the end of 2012, statistics for the United States estimate that 78 percent of individuals in this country are Internet users, compared to only 53 percent on Facebook.[45] Exact numbers are difficult to find, but it seems likely that nearly every household that is on the Internet is also on email. For particular demographic groups, especially younger people, email might not be their preferred digital tool any longer, but it is still used by every adult parishioner who accesses the Internet. Many adults who love Facebook or Twitter still check their email account more often than these social media tools because email is a critical part of their work lives.

Email is a good place to start and grow your digital outreach strategy. Beginning with a parish email communication initiative allows the parish to form its parishioners to expect that parish communications will now be delivered to them outside of the church on a regular basis. It can grow the number of parish families that connect digitally to the Church with a two-way communication vehicle. A campaign to grow the parish email list can be referenced later when you launch an initiative to encourage parishioners to become active on Facebook and Twitter. An email campaign, therefore, can be a great warm-up activity before launching a social media (Facebook, Twitter) initiative.

The Church (at least in the Northeast) has been slow to adopt email as a broad-based digital communication tool. We have been even slower in our parishes and dioceses to choose to use professional email services like MailChimp or Constant Contact to grow, design, manage, and analyze the effectiveness of our email communications. Here in the Archdiocese of Boston, we moved to email as a primary way for the central ministries to share announcements with parishes just two years ago. I am aware of only about a dozen parishes locally that utilize email regularly for broad-based parish communication and engagement. Every parish should embrace this way of communicating — it is efficient, effective, easy-to-use, and inexpensive.

Two examples of effective email communication are St. Paul's Parish in Cambridge's Harvard Square and the Church of the Nativity in Timonium, Maryland. My oldest son attends St. Paul's School, so we receive a weekly email each Friday afternoon with important announcements about the weekend's activities and a full copy of the digital bulletin. These emails are particularly helpful when there are street closures and events in Harvard Square that might limit parking, allowing us to plan to leave a little bit earlier. It can also serve as a good reminder to prioritize Mass in the plans for the weekend. The Church of the Nativity in Timonium, Maryland, sends out a daily devotional email at 5:00 a.m., entitled "Worship Fully Today." It contains a reflection of a verse of Scripture from Sunday's reading and then links to key ministries in the parish. Reflecting on the scriptural passage in the email is a good way to begin one's day.

FLOCKNOTE — A COMMUNICATION SYSTEM DESIGNED FOR CATHOLIC PARISHES

Flocknote is an online communications system that has the capability of sending email newsletters, text messages, phone calls, and social media updates for the entire parish and for individual ministries. Parishioners can choose to receive emails and/or text messages, and they can determine how many ministries or parish groups from which they would like to receive or share communication. For example, when an extraordinary minister of the Eucharist needs to reschedule his or her weekend, messages can be sent to all of the other members of the Eucharistic ministers list.

The parish (or ministry coordinator) simultaneously can send the same message out by email, text, and phone message, depending on the user preferences the parishioner has established. The objectives are to keep all parishioners informed, to begin the conversation with them about initiatives and projects, and to have a record of all the communications you have sent.

Flocknote also allows the sending of attachments, can allow the scheduling of notes to go out later, and can track statistics, such as open rates and email bounces (email addresses that no longer work). It allows recipients to reply back, begin a group discussion, reply to a poll question, or RSVP for an event — all without logging in.

Flocknote also allows parishioners to sign up easily on the parish webpage, in response to an email or text message. This can also help keep the parish-census database up to date.

There are six different pricing plans depending on the size of the parish, ranging from $7 to $160 per month. For more information, see Flocknote.com.

PRACTICAL SUGGESTIONS FOR IMPLEMENTING EMAIL COMMUNICATION IN THE PARISH

- **Conduct an email signup "campaign" period for two consecutive weekends.** Explain that you want to have a weekly email service that includes the bulletin and important announcements. Perhaps promote an important announcement that you will release by email on Sunday or Monday evening after the second weekend, to provide an even greater incentive to register. Repeat this sign-up effort each year in church, at ministry meetings and school gatherings, and in religious education. Attempt to include everyone associated with the parish in some way with the email campaign. Fall is often a good season to do this.

- **Sign-up for a professional email-management service such as MailChimp, Constant Contact, or FlockNote.** These services are worth the investment and have many benefits. One of the key features is that they help your emails avoid spam filters (particularly important when your email list is larger than 200) so that more of your emails reach their destination and get read. They also make it easy for parishioners to register for parish email lists on your website or to unsubscribe on their own without having to contact the parish office. They also allow the parish to have various and separate email lists for particular audiences (all-parish, school, religious education families, lectors, extraordinary ministers of the Eucharist, and so on).

- **Watch the great training videos.** Encourage the parish staff member with the task of publishing weekly emails (perhaps also the bulletin editor and website editor) to watch the training videos available on the email service you select. These videos will help the parish staff member to design, publish, share, monitor, and analyze email success to improve parish communications.

- **Create a template within the email program that you like.** Consider matching the graphics and branding of the parish website to strengthen the parish's digital identity. Try different templates, headlines, approaches, and email lengths and then ask parishioners for feedback on which ones they like better — it is an easy way to generate dialogue and to convey that this is about dialogue within a community.

- **Begin publishing the weekly emails, and ask a question at the end.** In the first few emails, the parish could ask, "What additional content would be helpful in this email?" Later, the parish can ask a thought-provoking question that highlights the upcoming Sunday homily or asks for a reflection on an announcement in the email. Analyze the reports on what percentage of parishioners opened the emails and what links were clicked on the most, to learn what engages your parishioners.

- **Place an email sign-up form on your website homepage.** Training videos from the email service provider will make it easy for your website editor. The email service likely also has cut-and-paste web code to help your website editor do this quickly.

- **Include a bulletin announcement promoting the email list.** Ask something like, "Are you receiving the weekly email from Holy Apostles Parish? If not, please visit HolyApostlesMytown. org and sign up in the box in the upper right. Our goal and hope is to connect with every adult parishioner through our weekly email to ensure that everyone receives the same information and to allow everyone to provide input to our parish staff on important questions."

- **Promote the email list within the church building.** Place a poster for the weekly email on church bulletin boards, and place a box with pre-printed email sign-up cards near it. Place pre-printed pew cards throughout the church, and ask parishioners to place them in the collection baskets each Sunday.

FACEBOOK FOR PARISHES

Facebook is like a bulletin board, where you can post updates on parish life, reflections on current events, photos, videos, links to interesting websites, and announcements.

Facebook's worldwide penetration of households and rapid growth is staggering. Worldwide, Facebook reached one billion users on October 4, 2012, and on March 31, 2014, it reported 1.28 billion users.[46] Less than six years earlier, Facebook only had 100 million users.[47] Within the United States, there are 166 million Facebook users (52.9 percent of the population), about two-thirds of the total population on the Internet.[48] Facebook reports that 59 percent of its users worldwide (655 million of 1.11 billion) access Facebook *daily*. In the United States, the average Facebook user likes 70 pages of organizations, non-profits, and religious organizations.[49] The average number of friends per Facebook account is 141.5.[50]

Based on these worldwide and national statistics, it is fair to estimate that about half of the average parish's adult parishioners are on Facebook. An average parish with one thousand adults would have a Facebook second-generation reach of 70,500 (1,000 adults x 50% on Facebook x 141.5 friends = 70,750 second-generation recipients). If only 14 percent of those who receive the second-generation message also share it, the original message would reach one million users — *for free* (except for the time invested).

Of the parishioners who are on Facebook, how many are utilizing it to evangelize, even if in soft ways, such as "checking in" at Mass? For those not yet on Facebook but on the Internet, the parish can help them connect with friends, relatives, kids, and grandkids by training them on Facebook and then encouraging them to tithe 10 percent or more of their social media messages or likes to faith-related content. The parish can also encourage parishioners to connect with one another on Facebook, not just with their friends from youth sports, universities, high schools, and the like.

One of the great aspects of Facebook is that you can share photos, videos, and links easily — and in fact, the more you share these types of links, the more they get read, liked, and shared. If a parish audio records or videotapes a Sunday homily, Facebook can be a great way to share it with so many people who otherwise would never hear the transforming messages proclaimed.

**LEADING THE WAY: INSIGHTS FROM
LISA TAYLOR AND SEAN ATER OF IMMACULATE
HEART OF MARY PARISH IN CINCINNATI
(FACEBOOK.COM/IHMPARISH)**

Immaculate Heart of Mary (IHOM) Parish has over 2,100 likes on Facebook as of November 2013. They post on Facebook, on average, five times a week, including prayers, faith reflections from publications such as *Magnificat*, profiles and images of the saint of the day, Scripture quotes, short selections from the *Catechism of the Catholic Church*, meeting reminders for their 100-plus ministries, links to Catholic videos (such as musical performances or vocation stories), and links to news articles from major Catholic newspapers.

Question: Based on your parish's experience, what advice do you have for parishes that have yet to embrace Facebook?

Lisa Taylor and Sean Ater: BE NOT AFRAID! Yes, things can go wrong if you don't have people dedicated to monitoring and updating your page. But if you are serious about evangelization, and you want to build community, you must consider utilizing Facebook.

With that said, look before you jump into the world of Facebook. Ask yourself some critical questions first:

- How will the Facebook page fit in with your overall communication strategy?

- Who will administer the page?

- What content will you post?

- How will the page drive traffic to your webpage?

- How will you handle interaction on the page, both positive and negative?

- Do you have quality pictures for your profile and cover photo?

We took the time to think through and answer these questions before we actively launched our Facebook page. It is better to think it through on the front end, than to be playing catch up after the fact.

TWITTER FOR PARISHES

Twitter is a free online social-networking and microblogging service that enables its users to send and read text-based messages of up to 140 characters, known as "tweets."[51] Because of its character limitations, tweeting requires very little time to post short, pithy messages and links.

I have found Twitter very helpful in following many Catholic publications and bloggers to get updated news stories or commentary on public events. I also greatly enjoy viewing Twitter comments from like-minded fans of the Patriots, Red Sox, Bruins, and Celtics during big games.

For a parish, Twitter has many benefits and uses. A great aspect of Twitter is the ability to follow many Catholic organizations, publications, and trusted bloggers and then retweet a few messages per day to your parish followers and expose them to great content. Ideally, they will then retweet the message to their followers and allow the original message to reach a tremendously large audience. Encourage parishioners to follow one another on Twitter so that friendships can be formed and deepened.

Twitter can be tremendously useful for the parish's New Media Outreach Initiative because it allows a parish Twitter administrator to share great Catholic content from across the world with parishioners simply by following various Catholics (starting with @Pontifex and the local bishop) and Catholic organizations (such as leading and local Catholic newspapers).

> ## LEADING THE WAY: INSIGHTS FROM OUR LADY OF GOOD COUNSEL PARISH IN PLYMOUTH, MICHIGAN (TWITTER.COM/OLGCPLYMOUTH)
>
> Our Lady of Good Counsel Parish has 693 Twitter followers, as of June 2014, to complement its 3,000 likes on Facebook. The parish tweets on average about twice a day, including daily Mass readings, feast-day profiles, links to Catholic magazine and newspaper articles, links to the parish's blog or Facebook posts, diocesan announcements and press releases, inspiring videos, ministry/event promotions, retweets of posts from priest and parishioner Twitter accounts, book recommendations from the pastor, links to the pastor's radio show and to all the priests' homily podcasts, links to the parish's "Chapel Chat" videos, promotion of open Adoration times, explanations of aspects of the liturgy, links to the video recordings of RCIA presentations, and notes on upcoming funerals.
>
> The Twitter account was one of the main ways OLGC parish promoted its community-wide program of Alpha for Catholics in the fall of 2013.

Signing Up for Parish Twitter and Facebook Accounts

The format of a book makes it difficult to *show* the steps and the ease of signing up for a parish Facebook page and parish Twitter account. Textual descriptions alone will make the process seem more difficult than it is. I encourage you to view the videos on the companion website, ParishGuideToNewMedia.com, for guidance in establishing your accounts.

The website also has links to effective parish Facebook pages and Twitter accounts, links to articles that optimize your presence on these tools, lists of Facebook and Twitter profiles to friend and follow, and descriptions of related tools (like HootSuite) that make managing your social media outreach more efficient and effective.

What Should Your Parish Post on Facebook or Tweet?

- All your blog posts (see list of potential topics in Appendix IV).

- All timely parish information and news.

- Announcements and reminders of weather-related cancellations or schedule changes.

- Promotional messages for parish events and seminars.

- Short posts about the upcoming weekend liturgies and homilies — to create excitement and to remind people of the Mass in a positive way.

- Short messages of gratitude from the parish for the great turnout at Mass, great participation and singing, generosity in giving to the collection, excitement for a new parish initiative, and so on.

- Links or posts from other Catholic organizations in Rome, in the diocese, from nearby parishes, or from Catholic publications.

- All parish videos and slideshows.

- Questions to begin a dialogue or to request feedback. Topics could be things like "What was most memorable about yesterday's homily?" or "What was your favorite hymn from this past Sunday?" or "Can you help us get eight additional volunteers to help paint the religious education classrooms tomorrow?" or "Do you know a family that we can bring a turkey dinner to this Thanksgiving?" can generate responses.

LEADING THE WAY: INSIGHTS FROM THOMAS SANJURJO OF NATIVITY CATHOLIC CHURCH IN BRANDON, FLORIDA (NATIVITY CATHOLICCHURCH.ORG)

Nativity Catholic Church has 1,192 likes on Facebook and 168 followers on Twitter as of June 2014. They are one of the first parishes in the country to have an electronic outreach director, Thomas Sanjurjo.

Question: What practical tips do you have for parish postings on Facebook and Twitter?

Thomas Sanjurjo: A good deal of learning a media platform is learning how your audience engages with it. A lot of playing around and calculating will go into making a successful campaign. Don't be too anxious about an effort not being immediately successful, and be willing to change habits based on the interactions of your constituents. One of the best ways to gauge this is to have a "group page" on Facebook, all of the posts are time-stamped, so you can see when the most active people in your area of influence are on. You might already have a group page for your parish — many parishioners start their own. Just ask around.

Question: What are the best strategies/tactics to get parishioners to follow/like your social media accounts?

Sanjurjo: The very best way is to get the priest to mention the accounts often and to make sure that they are updated with important, and interesting, information. Even if the priest talks about the accounts, if they are stale, most people will not get involved. You'll also find that starting with a small core of people who know how to share posts and encourage others to get involved will return a tremendous amount more than just posting about the accounts in your bulletin or on your website.

Question: What do you consider the essential social media platforms that evangelizing Catholic parishes should be on today?

Sanjurjo: The two most important social media platforms for parishes to be involved with are Facebook and YouTube. Facebook is the most commonly used platform for a general demographic; it also has the best options for using ads, for sharing information, and for analytics. YouTube is important because it allows videos to be uploaded without having to learn a complicated media management system; the videos can also be shared easily to the other platforms that the parish might be engaged with (most of the time, even automatically). If a third option is being looked at, Twitter provides an easy platform that even busy priests can get involved with.

See ParishGuideToNewMedia.com for additional insights from Nativity Catholic Church and Thomas Sanjurjo.

Parish Training on Facebook and Twitter

For a parish to become an effective hub for Catholic new media and to utilize new media as a primary tool of the New Evangelization, the parish needs to offer training coordinated by its New Media Outreach Commission.

There are many considerations for the training:

- **Location:** Ideally, the training would take place in an environment where the participants can be on the Internet with their laptops, iPads (or other tablets), and smartphones. If this is to take place in the parish hall, perhaps the New Media Outreach Commission can ensure that the Internet is wired to the hall and that a wireless router is installed. Bringing Internet access to the parish hall would have many benefits down the road for future parish events. If the parish hall were not an option, other possible locations would be a local Catholic school, public school, public library, or local college that has a computer lab or a classroom with ample wireless access.

- **Trainer and associate trainers:** Technology training often involves demonstrations and direct assistance with the sign-up steps. Your lead trainer should be comfortable with the subject matter and the aspect of teaching, but this person doesn't need to be an "expert" as long as he or she is comfortable saying, "I will get back to you on that question next session." The trainers-to-participants ratio should ideally not be worse than 1-to-10.

- **Training topics:** Most trainers would like to develop their own format and approach for the training by consulting training videos online, books on the technology, or the materials on ParishGuideToNewMedia.com. Some topics for training sessions are:

  > Why is the parish embarking on a New Media Outreach Initiative?

  > Facebook and Twitter for beginners.

  > Signing up and completing your first post on Facebook and Twitter.

  > Sharing videos, audios, links, and photos on Facebook and Twitter.

> Finding relatives, individuals, and organizations to "like" and "follow" on Facebook and Twitter.

> Growing the number of people who follow your posts on Facebook and Twitter.

> Sharing content you receive with your network on Facebook and Twitter.

> Connecting with other Catholics in the parish and worldwide on Facebook and Twitter.

> Following Catholic publications, bloggers, and organizations that can help you grow in your Catholic faith on Facebook and Twitter.

> Connecting with kids and grandkids on Facebook and Twitter: what to do and what to avoid.

> Tithing on social media: Why committing to posting faith-related messages as 10 percent of your social media messages will bring more fulfillment to your life and to many within your social media networks.

> Helpful social media norms and guidelines.

> Open forum for questions about social media.

- **Format:** Weekly trainings for a particular 6- to 10-week season can be used to teach these materials. Weekly formats allow greater assignment of exercises between sessions but slow the full adoption of the tools.

- **Recordings:** To build momentum, training sessions ideally can be recorded so that those who missed a particular session can catch up by watching or listening to the recording, or reading through the training materials. The distribution of the training video on the parish blog, Facebook account, and Twitter account will also encourage additional people to come to the next session.

Regular updates from the commission on the training, the latest topics covered, and the growth in social media participation in the parish can be shared weekly in the parish bulletin and parish blog. This will encourage more parishioners to want to be involved over time.

SUMMARY POINTS

- Email, Facebook, Twitter, and other social media tools can promote content on your website and blog, point parishioners and visitors to content directly, and engage them in conversation with your parish community. All these tools are essential elements for implementing and maintaining the parish's outreach to those who need to hear the Good News.

- The tools of social media have developed significantly over the past several years and likely will continue to evolve. The principle, however, of using digital tools to direct traffic to your home base will remain.

- All the tools currently for sharing content and engaging in dialogue are free or inexpensive. The main obstacle to embracing these will never be money, just time. These tools are all straightforward and quick to learn, particularly with the resources available online at ParishGuideToNewMedia.com.

REFLECTION AND DISCUSSION QUESTIONS

What percentage of your adult parishioners do you think utilize the Internet? Email? Facebook? Twitter? Google+? Instagram? Other tools?

•••

What percentage of your adult parishioners are connected with the parish through Email, Facebook, and Twitter today? What percentage do you think *would* connect if there was a well-marketed, well-run campaign, along with a fun training initiative that first educates parishioners on how to utilize these tools for their own personal relationships and then connects them to the parish through these tools and encourages them to tithe a certain percentage of the messages to be faith related?

•••

How would you structure the new media training for your parishioner group? Would you train people of all different technological aptitudes together or separately?

•••

How well do you think social media can keep your college-age parishioners connected to your parish and the Church as they attend university?

Chapter Ten

ELECTRONIC GIVING AND THE PARISH MISSION

"The Church needs to be concerned for, and present in, the world of communication, in order to dialogue with people today and to help them encounter Christ. She needs to be a Church at the side of others, capable of accompanying everyone along the way. The revolution taking place in communications media and in information technologies represents a great and thrilling challenge; may we respond to that challenge with fresh energy and imagination as we seek to share with others the beauty of God."[52]

POPE FRANCIS, MESSAGE FOR THE 48TH WORLD COMMUNICATIONS DAY, JANUARY 24, 2014

Once your parish embraces the call to become a hub of Catholic new media, it is inconsistent not to have a strong electronic giving (e-giving) option. Just as those who financially support the parish through e-giving are more likely to connect through new media, so too is the reverse — those who connect with the parish through new media are more likely to offer financial support through e-giving.

While new media tools are a growing and significant way for people to communicate and build community, online bill-pay and electronic transactions are becoming the preferred way that people choose to pay for life's expenses and to support charities of choice. Parishioners should have the opportunity to support their parish in the same way. There are many benefits to the parish and the parishioners.

E-COMMERCE

Are you writing as many checks as you used to?

Perhaps you are like me. In the past twelve months, I have written only 19 checks (an average of fewer than two checks per month). All of my other payments are done through my banks' online bill-pay system or by credit/debit card. I have found this to be more efficient, easier to track, cheaper, and quicker to integrate into our family budgeting system.

Nationally, statistics from the Federal Reserve show an increasing percentage of payments being made electronically each year, either through online bill-pay, credit and debit cards, or EFTs/ACHs (electronic funds transfers through the Automated Clearing House). The Federal Reserve's Payments Study found that 15 percent of non-cash payments in 2012 were done by check, down from 32 percent checks in 2006.[53] (Note: Percentages for 2012 do not add up to 100 percent due to rounding.)

Payment Type	2012	2009	2006
Debit Card	38%	35%	26%
Credit Card	21%	20%	23%
ACH	18%	18%	15%
Pre-Pay	7%	5%	4%
Check	15%	22%	32%
Total	**100%**	**100%**	**100%**

Over the past decade, many parishes across the country have chosen to offer an e-giving program to their parishioners. The adoption of e-giving as a way to support the parish, however, has also been mixed in many parishes, usually reflective of the way it has been marketed, the ease of switching from conventional methods of contributing, and the control that parishioners desire to make changes directly with their contributions. I will share more on this topic later.

An Evolution in Practical Financial Stewardship

Electronic contributions are an evolution from the way Catholics have practiced stewardship through the centuries. Stewardship involves the recognition that our blessings come ultimately from God and that God calls us to share these blessings with those in need, particularly through the Church.

Roughly 50 years ago, the concept of weekly collection envelopes took hold because most working Catholics were paid weekly, causing them to manage their finances on a week-to-week basis. This is generally not true today. Most companies pay employees either one or two times per month and many households plan their expenses monthly or even annually, driven by mortgage payments, car payments, utility bills, or large annual (or semi-annual) bills like taxes and tuition. Many Catholics report carrying less cash than they did 10 years ago, relying instead on credit cards, debit cards, and more frequent trips to the ATM for daily expenses.

The concept of e-giving is an attempt to update the way we encourage Church support. It integrates Church support into the way many Catholics are managing their finances and allocating their resources — with a portion reserved to share with others and give back to God.

> ### LEADING THE WAY: INSIGHTS FROM DEACON JIM KITCHENS OF ST. ELIZABETH ANN SETON PARISH IN FORT WAYNE, INDIANA (SEASFW.ORG)

Question: What did you do to promote e-giving and to maximize parishioner enrollment?

Deacon Kitchens: Initially we had an information session after all five Masses. We explained the process and how to set it up. Our priests spoke of it in parish announcements for every Mass for a month. We made handouts from Our Sunday Visitor available and still do. We also highly encourage it within our website, new-parishioner welcome packages, and in all giving statements that go to our parishioners.

Question: What have been the results of the e-giving campaign?

Deacon Kitchens: We currently have 381 families who use online giving as of November 2013. We would like to get this to 500. As well, we are in the beginning of a $9,500,000 Capital Campaign, and we are using online giving as a means to complete a three-year pledge.

Question: What feedback from your parish community have you received about your e-giving program?

Deacon Kitchens: Feedback is very positive. Several families really prefer to use credit cards, and this allows them to accumulate points. We have almost zero complaints, as the system and process is safe. The parish has received an enormous benefit. Our collections are up considerably since online giving was introduced. Many of our folks are absent in the summer, going to the lake areas. Our giving in the summer has been as strong as it is in the fall and winter. It has stabilized our income dramatically.

Question: How much time/work does it take to manage the e-giving program?

Deacon Kitchens: It requires less than 15 minutes each Monday to bring in the e-giving gifts into our systems and parish reporting. For the month-end close, we spend perhaps 30 minutes processing month-end online giving.

Question: Any general advice or best practices that you would recommend to parishes that might launch an e-giving program?

Deacon Kitchens: If your parish is like ours, with many young families that pay bills electronically, there will be no problem introducing it. Actually, young families are demanding it. For others, I would recommend addressing the fears that come about using technology to pay bills and make donations. Testimonials help, as do demonstrations that explain how it encourages stewardship. One thing we strongly believe is that even if online giving is their payment method, we encourage them to place a giving envelope in the offering each Sunday. The cost of envelopes is well worth the visible action of giving.

See ParishGuideToNewMedia.com for additional insights from St. Elizabeth Ann Seton Parish.

PARISHES AND PARISHIONERS WIN WITH E-GIVING

For parishioners, electronic giving can be much more convenient, allowing us to demonstrate a consistent commitment to our parishes, and enabling us to be reflective, not reflexive, in our support of the Church.

Let me illustrate this last point. Prior to signing up for traditional envelopes, "Joe Parishioner" put cash in the collection basket. If Joe intended to contribute $10 but in his pocket only had a $1 and a $20 bill, Joe faced a tough ("reflexive") choice about which amount to give. After signing up for parish envelopes, Joe typically now writes checks for the first and second collections on Sunday morning before heading to church.

But what if his family travels? Typically, Joe's family would not remember to bring the previously unused envelopes with the usual amounts to church to make up for missed collections in recent weeks. This led to a pattern where Joe, and many like him, contributes almost a "seat fee" to whichever church he attends, instead of making a commitment to support his home parish with regular, consistent giving, whether he is able to attend Mass at his parish or not.

Because Americans travel more than they used to, parish collections experience increased variability. It is a fair estimate that regular Mass attendees attend 40 to 45 Masses a year at the parish where they are registered. This has a detrimental impact upon parish finances because of the weekly collection variability and lack of predictability. As many families know, it is tough to make longer-term financial plans if you do not know how much income you can expect in a given week or month.

With e-giving, parishioners commit to a level of sustained support to their parish. They choose the interval — monthly, quarterly, semi-annual, or annual — that is convenient and budget friendly for them. This then becomes a "reflective" decision, made in consideration of other gifts, expenses, and bills, versus a "reflexive" decision on the Sunday during Mass.

For parishes, the benefits of e-giving are many. The major benefit is that parish income is much more consistent, sustained, and predictable. Parishioners make a monetary commitment to the parish and fulfill this commitment through an electronic system that ensures the parishioner's account is charged on a set schedule and that deposits are made into the parish's account according to that same schedule.

In most cases, parish income increases because parishioners continue to support their parish even when they are not physically present, due to illness, travel, weather, or the like. It also simplifies the work required to keep accurate records of donations and to provide annual contribution statements to each parishioner (now required by the IRS to take deductions).

A table summarizing the benefits of e-giving is on page 132.

Marketing Your E-giving Program

After you have gone through the process of establishing an e-giving program, you are about halfway to your goal. In most parishes, e-giving is not like the movie *Field of Dreams*, that "if you build it, they will come." You need to market and encourage parishioners multiple times in multiple ways to give it a try. That seems like it could be a lot of work, but if you plan to do this at the beginning of the program, and to repeat messages, it is manageable.

There are some basic steps involved in having a successful marketing (or re-marketing) of an e-giving program:

- Have a **launch weekend**, which includes a **brief two-minute talk** by a commission member or the pastor about this preferred

Parishioner Benefits	Parish Benefits
• Eliminates the need to write checks.	• Increased revenue and greater consistency in parishioner giving.
• Aligns financial giving to the parish with the family's income schedule.	• Reduced parish workload and data entry of gifts.
• Convenient when traveling.	• Savings on printing traditional collection envelopes.
• Full donation history available online.	• Alignment with Church teaching on stewardship.
• Printable tax receipts on demand.	• Greater transparency and enhanced internal controls due to reduction in amount of loose change and cash contributions.
• Email reminders of scheduled donations.	
• Personal flexibility to adjust contribution amount.	• Stabilized collections, which allow for better forecasting and budgeting.
• Easier to maintain an electronic family budget.	• Automated tax statements to parishioners.
• Comfort of knowing that you are practicing stewardship by supporting your parish even when unable to attend Mass.	• Ease of managing special and second collections.
	• Aligned with emerging e-commerce trends and preferences among parishioners.
	• Opportunity to attract greater financial support from younger parishioners, as giving is aligned with their financial practices.

method of support, the reasons it benefits the parish, and the many benefits for parishioners. Include a bulletin column (similar to the one below). Have some posters or pew cards available. Ask every parishioner who pays his or her bills online, or who conducts electronic transactions at places like Amazon.com, to give it a try for six months to help the parish.

- **Educate parishioners often.** Share information at least monthly on the progress of the program, on the reasons why it is helpful to both parishioners and the parish, and restate the request that every parishioner who pays bills online or makes online credit card transactions give it a try for six months.

- **Thank enrollees often.** In the parish bulletin, express gratitude for the increasing number of families that enroll in the program bulletin. Perhaps publish the number of parish families enrolled in e-giving as part of a weekly stewardship report, highlighting both participation and dollar results for this subset of total financial giving.

- **Ensure that there is a visible way for parishioners participating in e-giving to still partake in the ritual of the passing of the parish collection basket.** Have cards at the back of church or provide paper forms for parishioners to use when the collection basket is passed that say, "I support my parish through e-giving."

SAMPLE E-GIVING IN-CHURCH PROMOTION SCRIPTS

COMMISSION MEMBER

Good morning. I am Scot Landry of the New Media Outreach Commission. After talking with members of the Commission, today I am excited to announce the launch of our new e-giving program, which can help our parish tremendously. It can also make it much more convenient for each of us to support the parish.

It helps Holy Apostles by increasing the stability of our collections, making it easier to budget and to process contributions. It also saves the parish on the printing costs of the traditional collection envelopes. For parishioners, e-giving is convenient, it eliminates the need to write checks, and it provides a downloadable donation history at tax time. It is also very easy to sign up.

I would like to ask every adult in the parish, if you pay your bills online or use your credit card for online transactions, to give this program a try for six months. If it doesn't work for you after six months, please move back to the traditional envelope system. Please use the form in church today to sign up or register online on the parish website when you return home. I am available for questions after Mass, and there is more information in today's bulletin. Thanks in advance for giving our new e-giving program a try. It will really help the parish, and I think you will really like it too.

PASTOR

Today, Holy Apostles Parish is beginning a new initiative — our e-giving program. It can help the parish tremendously, and we believe it has many benefits for all our families. I am so grateful for your generous support of Holy Apostles, as it moves me to see the sacrifices people make so that we can reach out to those in need and to help one another grow as Christ's followers. Whatever way you choose to offer your financial support to the parish, I remain ever thankful.

I would like to ask every adult in the parish, if you pay your bills online or use your credit card for online transactions, to give this new program a try for six months. If it doesn't work for you after six months, please move back to the traditional envelope system. I have confidence that our new e-giving system will increase the stability of our collections, making it easier to process contributions and more wisely budget for the future of the parish. It also saves us on the printing costs of traditional collection envelopes. For families in the parish, e-giving is convenient, as it eliminates the need to write checks, and it provides a downloadable donation history at tax time. It is also very easy to sign up.

Please use the form in church today to sign up or register online on the parish website when you return home. I am available for questions after Mass and there is more information in today's bulletin. Thanks in advance for giving our new e-giving program a try. It will really help the parish, and I think you will really like it too.

Here is a sample bulletin message from a pastor to his parishioners.

●●●

WHAT IS THE BEST METHOD TO FINANCIALLY SUPPORT OUR PARISH?

I am so grateful for your generous support of our parish. It moves me to see the sacrifices people make so that we can reach out to those in need and to help one another grow as Christ's followers.

Is there a "best" method to financially support our parish? The answer, generally, is yes. In stating this, I wish to emphasize that this preferred method might not be best for *you*, and I encourage you to continue supporting the parish the way you currently are if it works well for you.

Here is a "general" list of methods people use to financially contribute to the parish. I have listed them in preferred order from the parish's perspective. Please consider giving the top options a try if you are open to making it easier on us in the parish office.

1. **Participation in the parish's electronic giving program:** Electronic gifts made through this system are the most convenient gifts for the parish to process and the most consistent for parish budgeting. Most of the people enrolled in this option have a credit card charged monthly or a bank check automatically provided to the parish each month. It is very simple to enroll and takes nearly no time after enrollment. The parish saves on processing time, envelope printing, and sending charitable-contribution statements for your taxes, as these are easy to print directly from your online account. If you pay your bills online or make online credit card purchases, I ask that you consider at least trying this system for six months. It would help us a lot.

2. **Monthly or weekly e-check from your bank:** If you do not want to enroll in the electronic giving program but instead pay your

bills in an online system from your bank, please consider creating a recurring weekly or monthly contribution to the parish and notifying us so that we can stop printing your traditional collection envelopes.

3. **Monthly or weekly check in traditional parish envelopes:** We encourage you generally, in planning your support to the parish, to consider your monthly bills and pray about how support of our parish fits into your monthly budget. If you pay most of your bills monthly, you might want to contribute to our parish on a monthly basis too, instead of weekly. If you prefer to contribute weekly by check, please know we remain grateful for your support in using this option. Checks still provide natural receipts, and although less convenient than e-giving contributions, they are certainly more easily accountable for the parish to record and process than simple cash contributions.

4. **Cash, in traditional parish envelopes:** Cash contributions require additional processing controls and, for that reason, are less preferable to checks.

5. **Loose cash:** We are grateful to all who support the parish through loose cash in the collection basket. Although this form of support may be the simplest way for parishioners to give, it is very unstable, and it doesn't allow us to budget or meet accounting and reporting standards as requested today. It also does not afford the parish the opportunity to provide you a statement of your contributions for tax purposes at the end of the year. If you are choosing to contribute loose cash because you want your contributions to be anonymous, please know that you can select the "anonymous" option in our e-giving program and maintain anonymity and confidentiality in your giving.

I would be grateful if you would prayerfully reflect upon your current method of financial support to our parish and determine if you might be willing to give our e-giving program a try. Thanks again for your stewardship of our parish and for your support of our many ministries. God bless you.

•••

SETTING A GOAL

It takes time to get everyone in your parish enrolled. With many initiatives in the Church, and with busy lives in general, it is common that parishioners need to be asked at least three times, often in three different ways, to take action.

The important thing with any initiative that can help your parish is to set a goal and keep trying to reach or exceed it. A chart like the one below might help you track your progress. I have filled in the results from a hypothetical parish.

Percent of families contributing by:	Current	1-year	2-years	3-years
E-giving program	0%	25%	50%	60%
Online bill-pay from bank	5%	5%	5%	5%
Traditional envelopes — check	40%	35%	25%	15%
Traditional envelopes — cash	10%	10%	5%	5%
Loose checks	10%	5%	5%	5%
Loose cash	20%	10%	5%	5%
No contribution	15%	10%	5%	5%
Total	**100%**	**100%**	**100%**	**100%**

LEADING THE WAY: INSIGHTS FROM JUNE BEERS OF ST. GEORGE PARISH IN NEWNAN, GEORGIA (STGEORGENEWNAN.ORG)

June Beers, business manager: We started promoting our online giving program about six weeks before we launched the program with posters, which generated talk and questions — more than I ever expected. We ran weekly bulletin announcements for four weeks with various phrases such as, "Forgot your checkbook or envelopes again? Online Giving coming soon!" We included the Online Giving Logo in each bulletin announcement. On the Sunday before we rolled out the program to the parishioners, I spoke after each Mass, explaining the program, the different ways of giving online (credit cards or bank transfers), and the benefits of giving online, to both parishioners and to our parish. After Mass, I handed out Our Sunday Visitor pamphlets, which gave directions to our website for signing up.

We had 34 parishioners enrolled at the end of that first month. Today we have 170 parishioners enrolled in Online Giving. That is 35 percent of all our givers. Those that contribute online have substantially increased their financial support to the parish — most have increased their giving 25-35 percent.

After I gave one of my promotional talks, the first comment I heard was simply, "Finally!" It made me smile. Other parishioners have mentioned the convenience of the program. We are a parish of predominantly middle-aged to older parishioners. Some of them are retired and often travel for many weeks to visit friends and family. Several of those families have commented that it is so nice not to have to worry "making up" their donations because they have set up "recurring donations" through online giving.

Parishes that want to launch an e-giving program should make a plan. Know your rollout date, and only make the e-giving link functional on that date. I think it is important that someone who is enthusiastic about the program speak with the parishioners after all the Masses the Sunday prior to opening your enrollment link and be available to answer any questions after Mass. After the first several months, speak with all parishioners again after Mass, and later at the one-year mark to let them know how you are doing. Each time that I have spoken (three times now), we have added at least 20 new online givers within the month. We put Online Giving pamphlets in our parishioner registrations packet, and we are still advertising with the Online Giving logo in our bulletin as well as publishing our Online Giving contributions weekly in the bulletin. Advertise, advertise, advertise the program. It is impossible to advertise too much!

See ParishGuideToNewMedia.com for additional insights from St. George parish.

ACTION STEPS

- Contact your diocese to see if it has a recommended or approved list of e-giving providers. If not, start with the programs from

Our Sunday Visitor, ParishPay, Faith Direct, and Liturgical Publications.

- Compare the programs and select the one that best fits your parish.

- Work with the vendor to prepare for the launch of the program integrating e-giving into your website.

- Announce the program to your parishioners in church, in the parish bulletin, through materials in the pew, and perhaps through a letter mailed home to each parishioner.

- Communicate progress as families enroll in the program.

SUMMARY POINTS

- Electronic giving (e-giving) has many benefits for parishes and parishioners. It is a critical service that should be integrated into the parish website. The e-giving option is consistent with a new media approach to growing discipleship and stewardship.

- For parishes, the benefits are increased revenue, greater stability of collections, reduced staff workload, savings on printing costs, better controls, and the fact that you have a "modern" way of receiving collections that aligns with the way many parishioners financially manage their family resources.

- For parishioners, the benefits are the convenience of not writing checks, having printable tax receipts on demand, and the ease of integration with family electronic budgeting systems. Plus, many parishioners simply want to help the parish, and this provides them a new way to lessen the burden on the parish office.

- Establishing an e-giving program gets the parish halfway to the goal. The other major element is ongoing promotion of the program by launching it in a big way, recognizing the growth, and continually asking parishioners to give it a try. Communicate that there is a preferred method from the perspective of the parish for parishioners to provide financial support.

REFLECTION AND DISCUSSION QUESTIONS

How did you come to choose the method that you use to financially support your parish?

•••

Has your financial support to your parish been a result of a "reflective" or "reflexive" decision, or simply a habit formed over time?

•••

If your parish has an e-giving program, how well has it been marketed and promoted?

•••

What could and should be done to encourage parish families to support their parish through an electronic (e-giving) program?

Conclusion:

GROWING THE CHURCH THROUGH NEW MEDIA

"Evangelizing presupposes a desire in the Church to come out of herself. The Church is called to come out of herself and to go to the peripheries, not only geographically, but also the existential peripheries: the mystery of sin, of pain, of injustice, of ignorance and indifference to religion, of intellectual currents, and of all misery.... Thinking of the next pope: He must be a man who, from the contemplation and adoration of Jesus Christ, helps the Church to go out to the existential peripheries, that helps her to be the fruitful mother, who gains life from 'the sweet and comforting joy of evangelizing.'"[54]

CARDINAL JORGE MARIO BERGOGLIO, ARCHBISHOP OF BUENOS AIRES, ADDRESS TO THE GENERAL CONGREGATION OF CARDINALS THREE DAYS BEFORE THE CONCLAVE BEGAN THAT ELECTED HIM AS THE CHURCH'S NEXT POPE, MARCH 9, 2013

Before the cardinals of the Church enter a conclave to elect a new pope, they gather for a series of meetings known as the General Congregations. During these meetings, cardinals and other Church leaders make short speeches on the challenges they see and the particular characteristics they hope for in the next pope to address those challenges.

Very few people that followed the 2013 conclave closely predicted that 76-year old Cardinal Jorge Mario Bergoglio would emerge from the conclave as the new pope, mainly because commentators thought that the cardinals would elect someone younger to lead the Church through a period of reforms. Upon his election, many of those same commenters then pointed to his brief speech in the General Congregations three days prior to the conclave as a factor in his election.

In the excerpt above, taken from the notes of his address, on the topic of "the sweet and comforting joy of evangelizing," it is clear that the future Pope Francis was calling the Church, first, to be outward-focused, instead of inward-looking, and then to go further — "to go to the peripheries" of human existence and to meet people with the love of Christ and his Church. This approach challenged all people throughout the Church to leave their comfort zones and embrace evangelization in new and more effective ways. Pope Francis has continually echoed these messages in his words and actions since his election.

EVANGELIZATION IN NEW MEDIA WILL FORCE MANY OF US TO LEAVE OUR COMFORT ZONES

I realize that calling Catholic parishes and parishioners to embrace new media is taking many of them outside their comfort zones. For these Catholics, evangelization is not a natural activity. It is the top priority of the Church, however, and it's something we must do — and in this age of increasing secularism, something we must learn to do *well*.

Further, I recognize that challenging many Catholic pastors, priests, parish staff members, and older parishioners to embrace technology and new media calls them to proceed even further outside their comfort zones for the sake of the New Evangelization. I do this because I believe a **New Media Outreach Initiative will be**

the most effective approach to outreach and evangelization for the foreseeable future. When we face something we find difficult or new, it is helpful to do it in the company of others who are similarly learning or struggling with the task. There is strength in numbers, and we can grow in relationship with all those we interact with in the process. In a parish setting, it can bring the parish more closely together. That is why I recommend the formation of a new commission.

New media also has the great potential to strengthen intergenerational relationships within a family. A problem some priests have expressed to me can be stated like this: "Since my parishioners are older and few are on social media, I am concerned that a new media outreach campaign will not be successful given this parish's demographics."

My response to these priests has been to ask them if it can be turned into an opportunity the older parishioners would enjoy. A possible parish approach would be something like this:

> We are encouraging older parishioners to invite their kids, grandkids, nieces, and nephews to help them get set up on social media; in fact, our parishioners are actually asking their younger relatives to post faith-related messages on their accounts to allow conversations to begin with them about why it is important for the older parishioners to share those faith-related messages on new media. They have asked their younger relatives to help them get on social media and to connect with them, but a first fruit has been a beautiful discussion of the Catholic faith.

Those parishioners who are uncomfortable with social media can still utilize email to share the parish's blog posts and other messages. Every parishioner that is online can make a positive difference, in some way, in the lives of those they are connected with through new media.

One Soul at a Time

The individual behind every email address, Twitter handle, or Facebook profile is a soul deeply loved by God.

We each have relatives, neighbors, co-workers, and friends who are far from the love and truth of Christ and his Church. Without being too presumptuous, we believe as Catholics that it is likely their hearts may be restless until they reconnect with God. **Every single one of these individuals, these souls, are worth the risk** — the risk of personal rejection, the risk of embarrassment, the risk that they "unfriend" us on Facebook or "unfollow" us on Twitter, the risk that they ask us to not send them faith-related emails any longer, the risk that they might not invite us to their neighborhood party.

Why do I believe it is worth these risks? There are few things in life more fulfilling than being able to say that we played a part, even a small part, in someone's path to eternal happiness with God. Wouldn't it be great if someone we took the risk to reach out to became one of the great saints in the history of the Church and remained eternally — literally — grateful that we took the risk for them?

If we could help lead even one soul to reconnect with God, isn't that worth the "risk" of leaving our comfort zones?

Your Help to Advance the Ideas Set Forth in This Book

My deep hope is that this book contributes to the beginning of a new era in the Catholic Church, through each of its parishes. I wish that every parishioner will become an agent of the New Evangelization by embracing new media to meet people on the digital continent, even on its peripheries, and share with them the Good News in his or her own unique way.

In the United States, we have 17,644 parishes. I hope every one of them embraces the approach I am generally suggesting in this book. It takes many early adopters, however, to try these approaches, and then to share what works and what doesn't work with all of the other parishes that come after them. Would you help your parish to become one of the leaders?

Many resources are available on ParishGuideToNewMedia.com. My hope is that, through links shared by readers of this book, the content on that website can continue to grow and help parishes with the implementation of new media.

The Catholic community across the United States, structured in parishes, together can innovate the strategies and actions and share vivid examples of how to grow the Church through new media. Would your parish be willing to take on this challenge? Would you share your experiences of what worked well and what you would recommend others do differently?

May God bless you in your efforts!

Appendices: Introduction

My goal in writing this book is that many parishes will implement these new media ideas and see many who are lost return home to the Catholic Church.

My experience of working for the Catholic Church in one of the largest dioceses within the United States tells me that three hurdles need to be overcome to implement any significant initiative.

First is the hurdle of motivation to prioritize the initiative. It is my sincere hope that the first few chapters of the book made a strong case that the New Evangelization should be a parish priority and that new media outreach is a great approach to connecting with the lost today.

Second is the hurdle of a strategy to implement it well. I hope that the idea of a New Media Outreach Commission (NMOC), while new to parishes in the United States, is something that pastors, parish staff members, and parish lay leaders see as a good way to organize these efforts. The charters and activities will need to be modified for each particular parish situation, but I hope what I have described in the book will provide a helpful framework.

Third is the hurdle of particular tools, plans, and timelines. The tools have been discussed in Chapters 6 through 10. The development of project plans and materials can take an immense amount of time. As someone who has led many projects, I wanted to provide a lot of resources that can be starting points for every parish's NMOC. Of course, each one will need to be modified, but I hope what I've drafted in the appendices will save your parish's NMOC a lot of planning time so that you can move more quickly to implementation.

Many of these resources for the NMOC are lists, timelines, and guidelines. Because those things are typically read in a different way than the rest of the material in this book, I have placed them in the Appendix section. In these pages you will find:

- Parish action plans for the first 24 months and for a typical week.

- New media messages for various parish audiences.

- A tool for rating your parish website.

- Parish blog-post ideas.

- Links for connecting parishioners with the universal Church and other helpful Catholic resources.

- Ways to integrate new media outreach with other forms of parish communications.

- An example of social media guidelines and training others.

APPENDIX I

Parish Action Plans for the First 24 Months and for a Typical Week

I have shared many ideas throughout this book on how parishes can become a hub for Catholic new media and thus animate parishioners to become agents of the New Evangelization. Often the sheer number of ideas in a book such as this can make it difficult to determine where to begin. This chapter attempts to make that process easier by suggesting where to start and then recommending a sequence of practical steps.

Please customize this material for your parish. Each parish in the United States is different in its history, culture, resources, and current new media capabilities. Templates for customizing this timeline are available at ParishGuideToNewMedia.com.

Sample Two-Year Implementation Plan for the New Media Outreach Initiative

I recommend a two-year implementation schedule for an initiative of this magnitude because I assume that each parish will not want to rush its implementation of a New Media Outreach Initiative. Some parishes will choose to implement their new media initiatives on a shorter timeline.

Parishes are at different starting points. The schedule below, however, assumes that your parish has not implemented these new media activities yet or that it will want to significantly improve its presence in each of these areas. Your parish's staff and New Media Outreach Commission (NMOC) will want to determine the best sequence of these nine implementation activities for your parish community. I have developed the schedule to implement the nine activities in the sequence below.

NINE IMPLEMENTATION ACTIVITIES
1. Formation of the NMOC.

2. Parish-wide launch and description of the New Media Outreach Initiative.

3. Email sign-up campaign and daily email implementation.

4. E-giving campaign (implement solution on current website, promote parishioner sign-up).

5. New and enhanced parish website.

6. New parish blog set-up and daily parish blogging implementation.

7. Video or audio recording of Sunday homily and significant parish presentations.

8. Parish social media campaign (Facebook and Twitter).

9. Parish mobile-device campaign.

Each of these implementation activities likely involves training, first, of the NMOC and the parish staff, and then in some cases, education and training of the parish community.

Implementation can begin at any time, and generally I would recommend beginning soon after reading this book. For the purposes of the 24-month implementation calendar below, I began the implementation schedule in April, which would allow for the NMOC to launch its first major new media implementation activity in September.

I recommend that the NMOC form teams for the implementation of each activity and also have a team that develops communication materials for launch for each activity.

Please adjust the calendar as appropriate for your parish.

Month	Name	Actions to Promote New Media Outreach Initiative
1	April	• Parish staff reviews this book, one chapter at a time, sharing their individual answers to the discussion questions at the end of each chapter. • Pastor begins the process of recruiting the NMOC.
2	May	• **NMOC recruitment takes place.** • NMOC members read this book and meet several times to discuss their individual answers to the questions at the end of each chapter.
3	June	• NMOC agrees on a charter, sequences the various initiatives, and appoints teams and team chairs for each implementation activity.
4	July	• NMOC six-month terms begin. Charter and high-level information about the NMOC is shared with the entire parish before the summer season begins, to prepare them for sub-initiative announcements in September. • NMOC email-activity team begins a pilot of the email campaign. • NMOC communications team begins to develop the communication strategy and materials for the September rollout.
5	August	• NMOC email-team members continue to develop and refine the email campaign. • NMOC communications team refines the communication strategy about the overall initiative and the email campaign.
6	September	• **NMOC communicates the overall goals of the New Media Outreach Initiative to the entire parish.**

		• NMOC recommends that parishioners read this book and gather for book-club type discussions, with NMOC-appointed facilitators for different nights of the week.
		• Each parish ministry is asked to consider how it will implement the goals of the New Media Outreach Initiative in its work.
		• **Email team implements the email list sign-up on the last two weekends of September in church, in the parish school, in religious education programs, and in each parish ministry.**
		• NMOC e-giving team begins its work to implement an enhanced e-giving solution on the parish website.
		• NMOC communications team begins to develop materials for the e-giving launch.
		• NMOC website team begins its work.
7	October	• **Daily parish emails begin.**
		• Bulletin messages and in-church announcements encourage those who have not provided email addresses with materials or links to sign up.
		• **Weekly book club meetings begin to discuss this book** (and the NMOC's goals) in different groups (ideally one group during the day, one group in the evening, and one group on the weekend).
		• NMOC e-giving team pilots the enhanced e-giving solution.
		• NMOC communications team finalizes the materials for the e-giving launch.

		• NMOC member or pastor writes a bulletin column based on the sample in the e-giving chapter (Chapter 10), titling it, "What Is the Best Method Financially to Support Our Parish?" • NMOC website team continues its work.
8	November	• **E-giving initiative and sign-up is implemented**, including a brief talk by an NMOC member at all weekend Masses, based on the sample in the chapter on e-giving (Chapter 10). • Book club discussions on this book conclude. Groups determine if they want to read related books on evangelization.[55] • Bulletin messages and in-church announcements provide status updates on the email campaign and the early sign-up to the e-giving initiative. • NMOC website team continues its work. • NMOC recommends that an evangelization-related book from DynamicCatholic.com's parish book program be provided to all parish families at Christmas ($2 each).[56] • NMOC communications team prepares materials for the website launch.
9	December	• Pastor or NMOC member expresses gratitude to all parishioners who have signed up for e-giving and for the email initiative. • E-giving enrollment assistance is publicly offered on at least one weekend. • **The new parish website is launched one to two weeks before Christmas, with prominent welcome messages to newcomers and visitors.**

		• Parishioners are encouraged in the daily email to forward an invitation to Christmas Mass to their relatives, neighbors, co-workers, and friends.
		• Advent reflections are included in each daily email.
		• Books, from the DynamicCatholic.com parish book program, are distributed by the NMOC on Christmas weekend to all parishioners and visitors. Pre-printed stickers with a message from the parish or NMOC are placed on the book's inside front cover.
10	January	• NMOC six-month terms renewed. Other NMOC members can be added at this time. Celebrate this milestone and review how the early efforts have begun to strengthen the parish community.
		• **Pastor considers taking up a second collection to fund NMOC initiatives** (video recordings, blog, website enhancements, etc.)
		• Email team has a sign-up weekend for new parishioners.
		• Website team requests feedback from parishioners on the new website. Enhancements are made based on this feedback.
		• Blog team begins preparations to launch the parish blog on Ash Wednesday. Team members begin drafting messages and links for each of the 40 days of Lent.
		• Video- or audio-recording team begins work to record one Mass's homily (or webcast) on the First Sunday of Lent. They train a videographer and set a schedule for recording, editing, and web posting. They do a run-through (test broadcasts) on the two weekends prior to the First Sunday of Lent.

		• Communications team begins preparations for the launch of the parish blog and the homily recordings. • Social media team begins to pilot Facebook and Twitter accounts and develop training materials.
11	**February**	• Communications team implements communications about parish blog and video recordings (or online campus). • **Launch of daily parish blog on Ash Wednesday.** • Handout cards are distributed to all those who come for ashes to encourage Catholics to use the blog posts for daily prayer reflections throughout Lent. • **Launch of recorded homilies (or online campus) on the First Sunday of Lent.** Video or audio messages posted on the blog. If video is chosen, team determines whether also to post audio podcasts online for people to listen to during commutes to work. • All daily blog posts are distributed by email and posted on parish Facebook and Twitter to pilot audiences. • Twitter and Facebook team begins to pilot social media accounts and develop training materials.
12	**March**	• Parish blog posts and recordings of homilies continue, with messages distributed by email, Twitter, and Facebook. • Communications team surveys parishioners on all the new initiatives launched thus far by the NMOC and prepares materials for the launch of the social media training. • Social media team finalizes a training schedule and curriculum, to begin after Easter.

		• Blog and email messages promote the Sacrament of Reconciliation and encourage parishioners to invite relatives, neighbors, co-workers, and friends to Holy Week and Easter Mass. • Video- or audio-recording team tapes a special invitation message for Easter featuring the pastor and NMOC members, posted on the parish blog and distributed by email and social media to parishioners, who are asked to share with all those in their networks.
13	April	• **Social media team begins implementation on the Third Sunday of Easter.** Those familiar with Facebook and Twitter are asked to "like," or follow, the parish's accounts. Those new to social media are asked to sign up for training sessions. • Priests and deacons mention evangelization themes as they preach on the readings, particularly the Acts of the Apostles. • Email and e-giving teams are available after Mass to sign up any new parishioners or to answer questions. • Communications team reports results on parishioner surveys on NMOC initiatives in the bulletin and parish blog, thanking parishioners for their feedback.
14	May	• **Social media training sessions begin for six weeks.** Goal is to enroll all adult parishioners who are active online. • Blog posts continue daily, and they get shared also by email, social media, and RSS feeds.
15	June	• Social media training sessions continue. • Specific emphasis begins to encourage parishioners to tithe 10 percent of new media messages to be faith related.

		• Parishioners with smart-phones or tablets are encouraged to "check-in" on Facebook at Mass on Father's Day. • NMOC updates parish on all the progress made by the parish in the past year.
16	July	• NMOC six-month terms renewed. Other NMOC members can be added at this time. Celebrate this milestone and review how the NMOC's efforts have added to parish life. • NMOC evaluates progress against all key initiatives and plans to either renew communications on existing initiatives or to add new ones (mobile applications, Instagram, etc.)
17	August	• NMOC plans for activity to launch in October (e.g., mobile-app sign-up).
18	September	• NMOC re-communicates its goals and initiatives to the entire parish community. • NMOC assists with the registration process and email sign-up for parishioners, religious education families, school families, and all ministries.
19	October	• NMOC launches a new initiative (e.g., mobile-app sign-up).
20	November	• NMOC makes a strong effort to significantly increase the percentage of parish families enrolled in online giving. • NMOC recommends an evangelization-related book from DynamicCatholic.com's parish book program, to be provided to all parish families at Christmas ($2 each).
21	December	• NMOC encourages parishioners in the daily blog, email, and social media links to forward an invitation to Christmas Mass to their relatives, neighbors, co-workers, and friends.

		• Advent reflections are included in each daily email and through social media.
		• Video- or audio-recording team tapes a special invitation message for Christmas featuring the pastor and NMOC members, posted on the parish blog and distributed by email and social media to parishioners, who are asked to share with all those in their networks.
		• Books, from the DynamicCatholic.com parish book program, are distributed by the NMOC on Christmas weekend to all parishioners and visitors. Pre-printed stickers with a message from the parish or NMOC are placed on the book's inside front cover.
22	January	• NMOC six-month terms renewed. Other NMOC members can be added at this time. Celebrate this milestone and review how the NMOC's efforts have added to parish life.
		• NMOC plans activities for the next three-to-six months. It considers whether the parish should launch its own mobile application to unite all of its outreach efforts.
		• **Pastor considers taking up a second collection to fund ongoing NMOC initiatives** (video recordings, blog, website enhancements, etc.).
		• Email team has a sign-up weekend for new parishioners.
		• Social media team begins promoting a new wave of training sessions for Facebook, Twitter, and other social media.
		• Blog team helps develop new reflections for Lent.

SAMPLE WEEKLY IMPLEMENTATION PLAN FOR THE NEW MEDIA OUTREACH INITIATIVE COMMUNICATIONS

Consistent routines make it easier for parish communications. Consistency also creates expectations for parishioners in terms of what messages they will look forward to receiving and then sharing with their networks.

Parishes are unique, with different weekly schedules. Below is an example template of a weekly schedule for after the completion of the nine implementation activities. It assumes that the parish's daily blog will have a different theme for each day of the week. This template can be modified to fit the parish schedule.

Tools for customizing this weekly action plan are available at ParishGuideToNewMedia.com.

Day	Actions to Promote New Media Outreach Initiative
Monday	• *Blog content*: Post video, audio, or text of Sunday's homily with a brief conversational introduction. • *Outreach*: Share a blog post through email and social media and retweet Catholic messages. • *Bulletin*: Solicit final updates from NMOC teams (and other parish ministries) for inclusion in the parish bulletin.
Tuesday	• *Blog content*: Introduce a new family, thank particular ministry leaders, or pay a tribute to a long-serving parishioner. Also, you can describe parish goals or explain recent decisions. • *Outreach*: Share a blog post through email and social media and retweet Catholic messages. • *Bulletin*: Finalize bulletin and send to bulletin printer.
Wednesday	• *Blog content*: Share a Catholic resource (website, movie, event, song, art, photograph, quote, etc.), adding your personal reflections. Or focus on an element of the parish website or a parish norm for sacramental preparation and explain it. • *Outreach*: Share a blog post through email and social media and retweet Catholic messages.

Thursday	• *Blog content*: Profile a parish ministry or initiative, or provide an update on the NMOC. Share summaries of parish finance or pastoral council meetings. • *Outreach*: Share a blog post through email and social media and retweet Catholic messages.
Friday	• *Blog content*: Provide a link to the upcoming Sunday bulletin. Include a good story from parish ministry in the past week. Pick a Catholic prayer, share a how-to guide for a Catholic activity, explain an element of Church history, or take parishioners on a virtual tour of a small part of the parish campus. • *Outreach*: Share a blog post through email and social media and retweet Catholic messages.
Saturday	• *Blog content*: Include Sunday's readings, links to a couple of reflections, and one insight or response to a question about the Mass liturgy. (Pre-schedule on Friday.) • *Outreach*: Share a blog post through email and social media. If someone is available to monitor the account on Saturday, retweet Catholic messages.
Sunday	• *Blog content*: Share top Catholic news, papal homilies, or diocesan announcements from the past week through links. (Pre-schedule on Friday.) • *Outreach*: Share a blog post through email and social media. If someone is available to monitor the account on Sunday, retweet Catholic messages.

Any day	• Email and social media mentions:
	  > Any funerals (name and time, with a link to the obituary).
	  > Theme of morning homily.
	  > Prayer requests for certain individuals or needs.
	• Share and retweet messages that come from the pope, universal Church agencies, the local bishop, diocesan agencies, or Catholic publications.

SUMMARY POINTS

- Each parish is different and begins a New Media Outreach Initiative from a unique starting point. Regardless of where a parish starts, however, it is likely it can implement all the ideas in this book within 24 months.

- Parishes would benefit from sequencing all their new media initiatives and launching new ones approximately every two months, to not overburden the NMOC, parish staff, or parishioners. Each parish may customize the implementation activity sequence.

- Consistency in blog-post content makes it easier on those creating the blog and creates positive expectations on those receiving and sharing the blog content through email, social media, or directly accessing the blog.

REFLECTION AND DISCUSSION QUESTIONS

Evaluate the nine new media implementation activities above for your parish. Which ones have been implemented already? Are they strong or in need of improvement? Can the household penetration be improved? How would you sequence the nine activities in your parish?

•••

What is your initial reaction to the draft 24-month implementation plan? Does it seem too rushed, too slow, or about right for your parish?

•••

What is your initial reaction to the draft weekly implementation plan? How would you improve it for your parish?

APPENDIX II

New Media Messages for Various Parish Audiences

We begin new media outreach recognizing that we are reaching out to so many people at different stages in their faith journey. It is similar to the experience of priests and deacons preaching in the Church, trying to ensure that their homilies and messages have something for everyone.

Significant Diversity of Parishioner Experiences

Within our parishes we include:

- Ninety-year-olds and those as young as nine days.

- Daily communicants and those returning to the Church for the first time in years.

- Those who receive the Sacrament of Reconciliation frequently and those who have not received since their first confession or since confirmation.

- Those who were born, raised, and who stayed in the parish and those who are visiting or have just moved in.

- Those who came from great Catholic families, those who came from households hurt by Catholic leaders, and those who were raised in households suspicious of any faith.

- Those with a very strong Catholic identity and those who keep their Catholic faith totally private.

- Those of different types of ethnic backgrounds and first languages.

- Those with many friends in the parish and those with no friends (yet) in the parish (or any parish).

- Those who can teach the faith comprehensively and those who have no answers and only questions.

- Those who are striving for holiness and those who wonder if God can ever love them due to past actions.

- Those who have never had doubts about their faith in God and those who just converted after years of struggling with discernment.

- Those who are intentional disciples, there to worship, and those who come to Mass as spectators or fearful that if they miss Mass they will go to hell.

- Those who hope for homilies that will answer their questions and deepest longings and those longing only for the quickest Mass possible so that they can go on with their day.

- Those who read the Bible regularly and those who think Bible reading is just for Protestants.

- Those who pray from the heart and those who would not know where to start.

- Those who regularly read Catholic articles, papers, and books and those who have never read a Catholic publication besides the Church missalette and bulletin.

- Those who welcome others and those who feel unwelcome.

- Those working in nearly every occupation and those who have been unemployed or underemployed for years.

- Those who recognize that their talents and skills are from God and those who do not believe they have any skills of use in the Church.

- Those who look for opportunities to serve and those who expect to be served by those employed by the parish.

- Those who share their financial resources generously and those who prefer to provide only token support.

- Those who are generous in their praise of others and those who are generous only in their criticism.

- Those who rejoice at the arrival of newcomers and those who resent anyone who might be sitting in "their" seat.

Parishes are made up of all types of people at various stages of personal journeys in Christ. Parish communications have the goal of including everyone, striving to help each parishioner to become a growing disciple. Uniting all of these people into one community is not easy work, but Christ's desire that we all be one in the Church must start in our own parish communities.

SELECTING NEW MEDIA MESSAGES THAT APPEAL TO ALL AUDIENCES

When it comes to new media messages to those in our parish and all those we seek to reach through our parishioners sharing messages with their social networks, we must recognize that no message can move every audience. Instead, we can try to reach everyone through a variety of messages over the course of a month. Our main thrust should be to help them feel part of the community, communicate that we care about them, and acknowledge that we all are growing in faith and, like them, are not perfect.

As we express our teachings and activities through new media to our parishioners and to our networks, we realize that these messages will be shared with people who practice nearly every other faith or no faith at all. So variety of message is important. Some simple messages are important to emphasize and weave in regularly. These messages should be newcomer friendly and seeker friendly.

SIMPLE SAMPLE MESSAGES

- I am so happy to be a member of Holy Apostles Parish community. We like each other. I have met a lot of friends in the parish, and I hope to meet new friends.

- We go to Mass — and we enjoy it, because it helps us to grow.

- We are a community of sinners, who are all hoping to become the very best version of ourselves.

- We learn a lot from our homilies, seminars, and from our conversations with each other. We are always learning.

- We care about our community and want to serve to make it better for everyone. We take risks to do so.

- We are praying that newcomers will become part of our community and then serve in ways that they can do what they do best.

- We have many great small groups that allow us to discuss life's challenges together.

- We have many opportunities to provide input, and our opinions count.

- Our people are encouraging to each other. We are nice. When we fail at it, we apologize.

- Our parish has a bold vision to transform our community and build a civilization of love. We are part of a movement, not a museum.

- We care — about ourselves, about each other, about newcomers, and about our friends in our town.

- We have some greatly dedicated and committed people in our community, and we always need more!

- We love that we are connected with over a billion Catholics in our worldwide family and more than _____ in our local diocese.

- We have fun. We laugh. We enthusiastically celebrate parish and individual milestones. We take our mission seriously, but not ourselves.

- We discuss some of the biggest questions in life, engaging both faith and reason. We like tough questions.

- We have the courage to change, to be more effective at living the mission Christ has given us. Please join and help us in this effort.

- Some of us have been very far from God at earlier points in our lives, but our lives have been transformed by responding to his generous love. We are humble and see ourselves as works-in-progress. We promise to meet you where you are.

- Some of us sing poorly at Mass — the community not only is okay with that but appreciates the effort!

- We love people. People are our priority. Every single person matters to God and therefore to us.

- Newcomers come back to our parish on successive weekends. They invite their friends and neighbors too.

- We would love for you to visit our community.

During a normal week, there are great opportunities to reflect on parish events and send a message that highlights one of these simple messages. Because these messages are easy to relate to, and describe the parish at its best, parishioners will be glad to share them, even in a secular society that often makes it uncomfortable to share faith-related messages.

After beginning the process of sharing new media messages, we can begin to integrate more deeply Christian and Catholic messages from time to time, including the essential messages of the great story of Jesus' love.

THE TITHE

Parishioners on social media can be asked to commit (tithe) that at least 10 percent of their new media messages will be about faith. It is important that they find other worthy things to tweet about that match their interests so that people continue to stay connected to their social networks. Tweeting about town events, local sports teams, and family achievements, or funny moments or hobbies, as well as sharing photos and videos, are all great.

One practical and memorable approach would be to share or retweet at least two parish messages a week. So if the parish sends out three messages a day (21 a week), a parishioner that is active on social media would share two of those with their network. Or if parishioners are personally creating three messages a day, they might share two faith-related messages a week. These communications should repeat, in order to reinforce basic messages about going to Mass, enjoying the homily, the warmth of the community, and the like.

SUMMARY POINTS

- Because of the existence of various audiences in the parish, and even broader diversity within the social networks of parishioners, we want to vary the messages.

- Many of the messages, particularly at the beginning, should reflect general interests of our community — e.g., how we build great friendships and grow both spiritually and in human qualities.

- To our currently active parishioners, we want to share messages that help them to grow, to be intentional disciples and share the great story of Jesus. Some will not want to retweet these more deeply religious messages, at least at first, and that is okay. We pray that they will view these messages themselves and be transformed by them.

- Parishioners on social media should be asked to dedicate (tithe) 10 percent of their new media communications to faith-based messaging.

REFLECTION AND DISCUSSION QUESTIONS

How would you describe the diversity of faith backgrounds and experiences within your own parish community?

•••

Which groups within your community are not being reached by your parish? What do you think they think about the parish and its parishioners? Would the "simple sample messages" above be received well by those individuals/groups?

•••

Which demographic groups in the parish likely have more friends in the local area who are unchurched or are Catholics who frequently do not attend Mass? How can we encourage them to be active in the New Media Outreach Initiative?

APPENDIX III

RATE YOUR PARISH WEBSITE TOOL

CATHOLIC TECH TALK

www.CatholicTechTalk.com

#	Criteria	Points	Your Score
1	Someone clearly has in his or her job description the responsibility for maintaining your website.	+30	
2	Mass times are clearly listed on the homepage.	+20	
3	Church phone number is clearly listed on the homepage.	+20	
4	"Contact us" form or clickable church email address is clearly listed.	+10	
5	Map or directions to the church can be found within two clicks from the homepage.	+10	
6	Current copy of the bulletin is available for viewing or download.	+10	
7	Welcome message from the pastor exists.	+10	
8a	Staff listing is updated with current contact information.	+10	
8b	*Staff listing exists but is out of date (at least one person's information is wrong).*	-10	
9a	Calendar of events exists and is current (at least one event +/- 30 days).	+10	
9b	*Calendar of events exists but is not current (no events +/- 30 days).*	-10	

10a	News or blog section exists and is current (at least one entry +/- 30 days).	**+10**	
10b	*News or blog section exists but is not current (no entries +/- 30 days).*	*-10*	
11a	High quality, warm, and inviting graphics or videos are used on the homepage.	**+10**	
11b	*Low-resolution graphics or videos are used on the homepage.*	*-10*	
12	Liturgical ministries page(s) exists, with descriptions and contact names.	**+10**	
13	Sacrament page(s) exist, with descriptions and contact names.	**+10**	
14a	Link to the Church's Facebook and/ or Twitter feed exists; pages are active and updated regularly.	**+10**	
14b	*Link to the church's Facebook and/or Twitter feed exists, but it's not active or updated regularly (no updates within the last 14 days).*	*-10*	
15a	Podcasts or videos of church activities exist; content is relevant.	**+10**	
15b	*Podcasts or videos of church activities exist, but content is not relevant.*	*-10*	
16	Link exists to e-giving and/or donation opportunities.	**+10**	
17	Link exists to church's school pages (if applicable).	**+10**	
18	Capability exists to capture email addresses ("contact us" form, newsletter sign-up, etc.)	**+10**	
19	*A "click counter" appears on the homepage.*	*-10*	

20	Your church site has a mobile template that automatically detects smart-phones.	+10	
21	In Google, typing "Catholic Church" and the city in which you're located yields your church in one of the top three results.	+20	
	Total Possible Points =	**250**	

Your Score

0 - 100 points: Yikes ... it's probably time to get moving! Get together and discuss solutions that can make your church website fully functional and beneficial to your overall mission.

101 - 150 points: You've got the basic framework for a working website, but there's always room for improvement! Decide what's working, what's not, and assign tasks for web-team members to carry out. Need some help? Advertise in the bulletin that you're looking for volunteers to help get your website up-to-date.

151 - 250 points: Nice job! You've got a great website, but don't forget to keep updating your content! Your site should keep your members up to date, as well as inform potential members or visitors about your faith community.

Archdiocese of Boston — Pilot New Media
LIST OF WEBSITE ATTRIBUTES FOR PARISH WEBSITE EVALUATION

www.PilotNewMedia.com

Appearance and Navigation

1. Good/memorable domain name
2. Modern layout and look
3. Site name prominent
4. Inviting and well organized
5. Spacing, font size and web-safe fonts
6. Main navigation system easy to find/follow

7. Navigation buttons clear and concise
8. Photos (attractive, inviting, organized)
9. Clear path to parish information
10. Homepage easy to "skim"
11. Easy access to the depth of site's content
12. Design and layout works on various browsers and mobile devices
13. Adequate text-to-background contrast
14. Emphasis (bold, etc.) is used sparingly
15. Styles and colors are consistent
16. Promotional icons integrate easy
17. Site map provides easy access to all website information

Content and Information

18. Mass, worship, and Reconciliation schedule
19. Bulletin
20. Contact information (email, telephone number)
21. Parish address
22. Directions and map
23. Staff profiles
24. Welcome message and mission statement
25. Newcomers or visitors tab
26. "About Us" page, providing important links to other information
27. Mass readings
28. Parish events calendar
29. Social media presence (e.g., Facebook, YouTube) easy to find
30. Priest's homilies (text, audio, video) on parish blog.
31. List of parish resources
32. Content for all demographic groups
33. Catholicism basics and links to faith content
34. Logistical information (e.g., parking, handicap access)
35. List of all ministries
36. Parish-groups pages
37. Multilingual pages (if appropriate)
38. Annual reports
39. Clear indication of connection to archdiocese and universal Church
40. Parish history
41. Ministry schedules

42. Slideshows and videos of parish events
43. Faith-formation materials
44. New feed on Catholicism and local news
45. FAQs about Catholicism and parish
46. Links to online Catholic bookstores, gift stores, and faith resources
47. Catholic music-and-hymns links
48. Parish bulletin advertisers and sponsors
49. Facilities schedule (e.g., classrooms, chapel, hall)
50. All documents current
51. Date of last update (ideally at least once a week)
52. Online campuses and webcasts – such as live.ChurchNativity.tv or StMonica.net

User-Friendly Functionality and Technical Elements

53. Accurate listing on search engines (SEO = Search Engine Optimization)
54. Sign-up for parish email list
55. Electronic offertory
56. Interactive map
57. Parish social-media feeds appear on website
58. Plug-ins and widgets (to integrate external content)
59. Downloadable calendar
60. Blog
61. Downloadable sacramental forms
62. Register online (parish registration and for various events)
63. Online prayer-request submission
64. Discussion forums
65. Search box for website content
66. Analytics, such as Google Analytics, embedded on the site
67. Incorporation of accessibility standards to allow site to work for visually impaired.
68. No obtrusive ads and pop-ups
69. Reasonable load time
70. All links working properly
71. Flash and add-ons are used sparingly
72. Intranet or special login (if needed for parish community)

APPENDIX IV

Parish Blog-Post Ideas

1. Post a Sunday or daily homily (video, audio, or text).

2. Post a bulletin column or important bulletin announcement.

3. Explain elements of the Mass and liturgy. Many parishioners would appreciate and benefit from a refresher on the various aspects of Catholic liturgy. They might also like to read a "behind the scenes" account on how the music director selects the hymns, how the altar servers are prepared for their sacred duties, or the prayers the priests recite before Mass, inaudibly during Mass, or after Mass.

4. Describe a moving, inspirational, or noteworthy event (e.g., funeral, wedding, or baptism celebrated, interesting conversation with a parishioner, reaction about the parish from someone you encounter in town).

5. Update the parish on a big initiative, such as a capital campaign or outreach initiative (consider promoting that this will only be on the blog or be posted first on the blog, to drive more traffic).

6. Profile a parish ministry, your involvement with its members, and why others would benefit from joining it.

7. Teach about certain Catholic prayers.

8. Share great Catholic resources through a link and share personal reflections (e.g., if you have a Catholic radio station in your area, perhaps discuss your favorite program; or promote a great Catholic website, using a screenshot of its homepage as the image, and describe why you like it).

9. Request prayers for certain initiatives, needs, or individuals.

10. Share summaries of important parish council and finance council meetings (perhaps with a question to gather input for a discussion at the next meeting).

11. Comment on a Catholic book, movie, quote, event, song, piece of art, or photograph.

12. Introduce a new family with a photo, a little bit about them, and their first reactions to the welcome of parishioners.

13. Describe the norms and prerequisites for baptisms, marriage, funerals, and sponsor certificates. If these are already listed on your website, the blog post can draw attention to them, provide an introduction, and then link to them.

14. Promote the RCIA program, especially during particular seasons, and ask each parishioner to consider three friends or relatives to invite.

15. Share the bishop's appeal or collection materials. Parishioners can be inspired by the good stewardship and the positive impact their contributions (joined to the contributions of thousands of other Catholics) make.

16. Provide a how-to guide for a Catholic activity or practice (such as how to pray the Rosary, how to go to confession, how to examine one's conscience, how to make a great Lenten Friday meal, how to invite someone to return to church, or how to pray grace before meals with people of other faiths).

17. Describe a parish goal, and ask for suggestions on how to achieve it.

18. Pick a topic and provide a list of great resources (such as strengthening your marriage, raising great kids, picking an excellent Catholic college, finding a good retreat center, or traveling to Rome).

19. Answer questions. Undoubtedly, you receive questions each week that other parishioners would benefit from hearing the answers to. Blogs are a great way to aggregate several questions and then respond.

20. Explain the reasoning behind a parish decision.

21. Record and share a short video interview with a staff member, ministry group leader, parishioner, or visiting missionary preacher.

22. Describe important content on your parish website or the diocesan or Vatican websites.

23. Post (with appropriate permission) a letter from the bishop, a statement from the U.S. bishops' conference, or a papal document and provide comments and reactions.

24. Thank parishioners, initiative leaders, bulletin sponsors, etc., in a way that shows a general sense of gratitude to all parishioners.

25. Pay a tribute to a recently deceased parishioner for his or her life of faith.

26. Share links to the top three Catholic news articles or opinion pieces (of the past day or week) that you encourage parishioners to read. Provide a short paragraph of why you are personally recommending these stories.

27. Discuss an important, interesting, inspiring, or funny element of parish history, diocesan history, or Church history.

28. Publish the parish's annual report. (To increase blog traffic, consider publishing it first, or only, on the parish blog.)

29. Take parishioners on a "virtual tour" of a small part of the parish campus through photos, videos, and descriptive text. If you have a complete virtual tour on your website, focus on a particular element in your blog (perhaps a statue or stained-glass window of a saint on that saint's feast day).

30. Include guest posts, perhaps from nearby priests or from community leaders in your town. If they have a large social media following, this can help increase traffic to your new media platforms.

APPENDIX V

CONNECTING PARISHIONERS WITH THE UNIVERSAL CHURCH AND HELPFUL CATHOLIC RESOURCES

One of the key aims of this book is that parishes should become animating hubs of the New Evangelization so that parishioners will become effective agents of the New Evangelization.

A key step is exposing parishioners to great Catholic content through the website, blog, email, and social media. Here is a list of faith resources to include on the parish website, related Facebook links, and Twitter handles for the same organizations, and then Catholic mobile applications.

LINKS TO INCLUDE ON A "FAITH RESOURCES" PAGE ON THE PARISH WEBSITE

- **Parish-related websites:** Links to any external websites related to the parish, such as a Catholic school, mission project, youth group, and so on.

- **Parish-related blogs:** Links to any other blogs (beyond the official parish blog) associated with the parish.

- **Websites of nearby and bordering parishes.**

- **Website of your diocese.**

- **Diocesan ministry and initiative websites.**

- **Diocesan vocations office, general vocational discernment websites, and local seminary websites.**

- **Websites for Catholic secondary schools and Catholic colleges and universities in your area.**

- **Local pregnancy help and diocesan pro-life office websites.**

- **Statewide Catholic Conference (public policy) website.**

- **Universal Church websites:** Vatican.va, News.va.

- **USCCB.org and national websites sponsored by the U.S. Conference of Catholic Bishops.**

- **Apologetics websites** like Catholic Answers and StrangeNotions .com.

- **Bible resources** such as the Catholic New American Bible at USCCB.org.

- *Catechism of the Catholic Church* **and the** *Compendium of the Catholic Church* on Vatican.va.[57]

- **Mass resource websites.**

- **Catholic marriage and family websites:** ForYourMarriage.org, FathersforGood.org, Natural Family Planning,[58] TheologyOfThe Body.net, Retrouvaille.org, and Marriage Encounter (wwme.org).

- **Catholic men's and women's organizational websites** such as the Knights of Columbus (kofc.org) or the Catholic Daughters of the Americas (CatholicDaughers.org).

- **Prayer-resource websites:** FamilyRosary.org, TheDivineMercy .org, and comprehensive Catholic prayer sites.

- **Public issues and action websites:** Religious liberty, faithful citizenship, human dignity, and many other issues from USCCB.org.

- **Diocesan newspaper or magazine websites.**

- **Catholic news websites** such as CatholicNews.com, Catholic NewsAgency.com, Zenit.org, and NCRegister.com.

- **National and local Catholic television- and radio-apostolate websites:** EWTN.com, CatholicTV.com, and SaltandLightTV .org. If you do not have a Catholic radio station locally, provide links to EWTN.com/Radio, AveMariaRadio.net, and RelevantRadio.com.

- **Online faith-formation programs** like MyCatholicFaith Delivered.com.

- **Websites for the leading Catholic book publishers.**

Please visit ParishGuideToNewMedia.com for an updated list of websites with direct click-through links. There is also a list of Catholic blogs I follow. Some parishes will choose to include those additional resources. Others may want to include only those sponsored by official Catholic organizations listed in the official Catholic directory.

FACEBOOK PAGES TO "FAN" AND TWITTER PROFILES TO "FOLLOW"

Most of the Facebook pages and Twitter accounts I recommend following are those of the above organizations. I have included a large list of social media accounts at ParishGuideToNewMedia.com for Catholic publications and Catholic initiatives. This list will be updated regularly based on the suggestions of visitors and readers of this book.

MOBILE APPLICATIONS

There are many mobile apps parishes can encourage their parishioners to add to their smartphones or tablets. Most apps are not "officially" approved by the Church (at least not yet), but I have found them very helpful in my own journey of faith.

On the next page is a list of 50 of the most popular Catholic apps in alphabetical order. An updated list, with hyperlinks to the Apple and Android application stores, is available on ParishGuideToNew Media.com.

- Baltimore Catechism
- Catholic Devotions
- Catholic Handbook
- Catholic Mass Times
- Catholic NABRE Bible
- Catholic News Live
- Catholic Short Prayers
- CatholicTV
- CatholicVote
- Compendium of the Catholic Church
- Confession
- Divine Mercy App
- Divine Office
- eVotions
- FamilyRosary

- FOCUS Equip
- Fulton Sheen Audio Library
- Holy Sepulchre 3D Virtual Tour
- iBreviary
- iCatholicRadio
- iConfess
- iMissal
- Immaculate Heart Radio
- iPieta
- iRosary
- Laudate
- Magnificat
- Mea Culpa
- Missio
- Mother of Perpetual Help Novena
- My Year of Faith
- NAB Bible for BibleReader

- New American Bible RE
- The New Mass
- The Pilot
- Pope App
- Pope2you
- Prayer 2000+ Catholic Prayers
- Recordatio
- The Roman Missal
- The Rosary of the Hours
- Saint of the Day
- Scriptural Rosary
- Sistine Chapel 3D Virtual Tour
- 3 Minute Retreat
- Universalis
- Vatican Radio
- Wakeup to the Creed
- Way of the Cross
- Word on Fire (Father Robert Barron)

SUMMARY POINTS

- There are many wonderful Catholic resources that exist online, on mobile devices, and in social media. It is likely that many parishioners in every parish across the country are not yet aware of many of them.

- As a hub for Catholic new media, parishes can help parishioners grow in faith by listing these resources on their parish website, promoting these lists in the parish bulletin and blogging about them from time to time.

REFLECTION AND DISCUSSION QUESTIONS

What are your favorite Catholic websites and why?

•••

If you have a smartphone or tablet, what are your favorite Catholic apps and why?

•••

If you could design an app to help you grow in faith, what would it do?

APPENDIX VI

INTEGRATING NEW MEDIA OUTREACH WITH OTHER FORMS OF PARISH COMMUNICATIONS

There are many methods of parish communication. Ideally, all the communication methods align with one another. As a parish launches and grows a New Media Outreach Initiative, it is important that the existing channels of parish communication promote the new media tools and vice versa.

Here are some straightforward and simple actions to integrate and align the digital outreach with other forms of parish communication.

Parish Communication Channel	Actions to Promote and Integrate New Media Outreach
1. **Verbal: Preaching**	❑ Mention in homilies the New Media Outreach Initiative every time the Mass readings focus on evangelization. Share why your parish is conducting the initiative. Indicate that your hope is for 100 percent participation, in which all parishioners do their part.
2. **Verbal: In-church announcements**	❑ Have a brief announcement at the appropriate time when each implementation activity of the New Media Outreach Initiative begins or reaches a significant milestone (e.g., announce the beginning of the email sign-up campaign). Share progress reports and identify the next steps for all parishioners.
3. **Verbal: Parish meetings**	❑ Include a mention of the campaign (or a current implementation activity) and indicate your hope for 100 percent participation of parishioners.

4. **Weekly bulletin**	❏ Dedicate a prominent place in the parish bulletin for the New Media Outreach Commission to update parishioners, promote training, indicate actions, and request assistance. ❏ Ensure the website link, Facebook link, and Twitter name are listed prominently next to the parish phone number and email address. ❏ Include regular bulletin announcements promoting sign-up for the digital distribution vehicles (parish email list, website, Facebook, Twitter). ❏ Occasionally have a bulletin blurb from the NMOC asking something like, "How many messages did you forward this week by email, Facebook, and Twitter?"
5. **In-church brochures and pew cards**	❏ Print a tri-folded brochure or a two-sided, small pew card with information on the New Media Outreach Commission and the short list of steps you are requesting of each parishioner.
6. **In-church bulletin boards and posters**	❏ Place messages about the New Media Outreach Initiative on the parish bulletin boards at all church entrances. Focus on a key action step of the month for each parishioner.
7. **Promotion cards (business-card size)**	❏ Two-sided, business-card-size cards are typically less than a penny to print in large quantities.[59] These make great handouts for the pastor, parish staff, and New Media Outreach Commission members to distribute at all parish meetings and in meetings with parishioners. All the key new media outreach activities can be referenced on this card.

8. **Seasonal newsletters**	❏ If your parish has seasonal newsletters, include a full page on the background of the New Media Outreach Initiative, the progress thus far, and the steps for the next season. Perhaps also profile some of the members of the commission and have them share stories of the initiative, why they are excited to be involved, and what they ask of each adult parishioner.
9. **Fundraising appeal letters**	❏ Mention in the fund-raising letters how important it is to the pastor, parish staff, and parish leadership committees to listen to feedback from parishioners. Stress that dialogue/conversation is one of the main purposes of the New Media Outreach Initiative. ❏ Encourage parishioners to connect with the parish through email, Facebook and Twitter (by providing the links) and participate in the many conversations about strengthening the parish for the future.
10. **Annual reports**	❏ Provide a complete recap of the initiative and share participation metrics and other statistics from the various new media activities. ❏ Share statistics, contributions, and evaluations of the parish's efforts to increase the percentage of families giving online.
11. **Offertory envelopes**	❏ Place the parish website, Facebook link, and Twitter handle below the parish name on the front of the offertory envelopes. Include a sentence at the bottom, or on the back, such as, "Please consider supporting the parish through our online offertory program. Visit the parish website for more information."

12. **Religious education and school letters**	❏ Include the parish website, Facebook link, and Twitter name on the letterhead of the parochial school and the religious education office.
	❏ Place a P.S. in all letters, such as, "Father [name] has requested that every enrolled family connects with the parish through email, Facebook, and Twitter. Thank you to all the families that have already connected. If you haven't done this yet, please do so through the parish website."
13. **Official parish website**	❏ Place prominently on the homepage the icons for Facebook and Twitter (and any other social media). Or include Facebook and Twitter widgets that show those feeds directly on the website.
	❏ Add a prominent box for "Email List" sign-up on the homepage.
	❏ Add a page on the website about the New Media Outreach Initiative.
14. **Other parish websites**	❏ Request or require these other ministries with separate websites to have a prominent link to the official parish website, Twitter, and Facebook accounts.
15. **Parish blog**	❏ Include prominent links, icons, or widgets for the parish's website, Facebook, Twitter, and email sign-up form.
	❏ Write blog entries on any significant developments in the New Media Outreach Initiative.

	❏ Promote other parish communications from the bulletin, newsletter, in-church announcements, annual report, fund-raising-campaign letters, etc., through the parish blog.
16. **Parish Facebook**	❏ Include the parish website and Twitter name in the Facebook profile.
	❏ Mention any significant developments in the New Media Outreach Initiative or link to the blog posts.
	❏ Promote other parish communications from the bulletin, newsletter, in-church announcements, annual report, fund-raising-campaign letters, etc., perhaps by sharing to a blog post on the topic.
17. **Parish Twitter**	❏ Include the parish website and Facebook link in the Twitter profile.
	❏ Mention any significant developments in the New Media Outreach Initiative or link to the blog posts.
	❏ Promote other parish communications from the bulletin, newsletter, in-church announcements, annual report, fund-raising-campaign letters, etc., perhaps by sharing to a blog post on the topic.
	❏ For key messages, ask parishioners to retweet the message. For others, create a hashtag to draw attention (e.g., #New MediaOutreach).

18. **Parish email**	❏ Include a section within the email template for "Important Links." Include links to the parish website, parish blog, the New Media Outreach Initiative page, and other important seasonal links.
	❏ Include an icon at the bottom of the email to subscribe to the email list (this allows people who receive the message to also sign up).
	❏ Include buttons or links to "Like us on Facebook" or "Follow us on Twitter," which take people to your Facebook and Twitter pages.
19. **Parish photos and slideshows**	❏ Place a textual overlay with the parish website name, Facebook link, and Twitter handle on the bottom of the video (such as where television networks place their logo). If this is too difficult, add a slide at the end of the video or photo slideshow that communicates this information.
	❏ Share videos and photo slideshows on the parish blog (with commentary) and on Facebook and Twitter (with a short introduction).
20. **Parish videos and webcasts**	❏ Place a textual overlay with the parish website name, Facebook, and Twitter mentions in the lower third of the video or in a slide at the end.
	❏ Share these videos on the blog (with commentary) and on Facebook and Twitter (with a short introduction).

21.Parish audio recordings and podcasts	❏ Add a verbal introduction or ending to the audio file, such as, "This audio recording is brought to you by Holy Apostles Parish in [Name of the city]. Please visit us online at WebsiteName .com, and connect with us through Facebook, Twitter, and Email so that you can listen to more audio recordings just like this one."
	❏ Share these audio recordings on the blog (with commentary) and on Facebook and Twitter (with a short introduction).

Adopting Social Media Guidelines and Training Others

All of us in the Church want to ensure that norms and guidelines govern our prudential use of new media for evangelization in order to protect those who serve the Church, those we serve, and the many institutions of the Church.

In the Archdiocese of Boston, our general counsel's office (Beirne Lovely, general counsel, and Fran Rogers, associate general counsel) coordinated a process of gaining input from many of the offices of the archdiocese, including our Secretariat for Catholic Media, to write up parish and ministry guidelines for the use of social media.

I encourage you to check with your own diocesan offices for local policies. In the absence of written norms in your local area, you may want to consult with appropriate officials to modify these for your own use. At a minimum, these may provide your parish with some general guidance on the use of social media.

•••

The Archdiocese of Boston

GUIDELINES FOR THE USE OF SOCIAL MEDIA
May 9, 2012

Introduction

Go, therefore, and make disciples of all nations, baptizing them in the name of the Father, and of the Son, and of the Holy Spirit, teaching them to observe all that I have commanded you. (Matthew 28:19-20)

The Church exists in order to evangelize (*Evangelii Nuntiandi* 18). New technologies, new media, and the Internet in particular, offer tremendous opportunities and an equal number of challenges to those who take seriously the work of evangelization.

In his message for the 44th World Communication Day Pope Benedict XVI said:

> The world of digital communication, with its almost limitless expressive capacity, makes us appreciate all the more Saint Paul's exclamation: "Woe to me if I do not preach the Gospel" (1 Corinthians 9:16). The increased availability of the new technologies demands greater responsibility on the part of those called to proclaim the Word, but it also requires them to become more focused, efficient, and compelling in their efforts.

The use of technology is rapidly growing to form, inform and, with God's grace, transform the adults, teens, and children of our Archdiocese. It is important, however, that we make every effort to ensure the safety of producers and consumers of social media, while at the same time ensure the integrity of the message we proclaim. This requires responsible, focused, and intentional use of new and yet-to-be developed technologies.

Pope Benedict XVI has repeatedly recognized the significance of these new technologies and the benefits that they offer to all individuals and communities. At the same time, he has warned that in using the new digital communications that are available, they must be used in a manner so as to promote "*a culture of respect, dialogue, and friendship.*" For everyone's further appreciation and understanding of the role such communications play in proclaiming the Gospel, we recommend reading the Holy Father's messages for World Communication Days.[60]

These Guidelines spring from the questions and concerns raised by many throughout the Archdiocese and are the product of research and consultation with other dioceses, archdiocesan ministry and administrative offices, and parish ministers. They are offered as a synthesis of best practices, consistent with the United States Conference of Catholic Bishops' Social Media Guidelines. The USCCB guidelines are available at http://www.usccb.org/about/communications/social-media-guidelines.cfm and should also be consulted by anyone engaging in the use of social media. It is our hope and fervent prayer that these Guidelines will assist Church personnel as they use the new tools of technology to proclaim the Gospel.

Establishing a Social Media Site

These Guidelines apply to all Church Personnel within the Archdiocese of Boston who create or contribute to social networking sites, blogs, or any other kinds of social media. Examples of social media sites include YouTube®, Facebook®, Twitter®, Wikipedia®, MySpace®, LinkedIn®, blogs, and comments on any online media stories or articles. Other websites are usually not considered social media, but many of the principles contained in this document should also guide the creation and use of parish, school, and ministry websites. For the purpose of these Guidelines, "Church Personnel" are defined as bishops, priests, deacons, religious, seminarians, pastoral ministers, administrators, lay employees, officers, directors, trustees, governors, members, and volunteers (collectively, "Church Personnel") in our parishes, agencies, schools, and organizations sponsored by the Archdiocese or for which the Archdiocese or the Roman Catholic Archbishop of Boston (the "Archbishop") has the direct or indirect right (whether alone or in conjunction with others) to elect or appoint officers, directors, trustees, governors, and/or members (collectively, "Archdiocesan Affiliated Organizations").

GUIDELINES:

- All social media sites created on behalf of the Archdiocese of Boston, any of its parishes or schools, any ministry or department of any parish or school, or any other Archdiocesan Affiliated Organization must only be created and maintained by Church Personnel or third parties specifically selected and designated by the organization to create and/or maintain such sites.

- There should be at least two site administrators for each official social networking site. Site administrators must be adults and should either be Church Personnel or third parties specifically selected and designated by the organization to maintain such sites.

- To the extent possible, all social media sites established on behalf of the Archdiocese of Boston, any of its parishes or schools, any ministry or department of any parish or school, or any other Archdiocesan Affiliated Organization should be created using the official Archdiocesan, parish, school, or other Archdiocesan Affiliated Organization email address of a site administrator. An official email address may be the email address provided by the Archdiocese, parish, school, or Archdiocesan Affiliated Organization, or an email address generally used by the site administrator to receive Archdiocesan, parish, school, or Archdiocesan Affiliated Organization communications. Any email address listed on an official Archdiocesan, parish, school, or Archdiocesan Affiliated Organization website is normally considered an official email address.

- Passwords and names of sites must be registered in a central location, and more than one Church official should have access to this information. When a social media site is created and maintained by a parish, parish school, or parish or school ministry, the Pastor must have access to the password for the site and all other relevant site information.

- No personal contact information (for example, home phone numbers or addresses) should be listed in the profile fields of official social media sites. Only official email addresses, office phone numbers, and job titles should be listed.

- Although all Catholics are encouraged to be witnessing to their faith at all times, personal social networking sites should never be used for official ministerial purposes. Personal sites may refer people to official sites of the Archdiocese of Boston, any of its parishes or schools, any ministry or department of any parish or school, or any other Archdiocesan Affiliated Organization.

- All information displayed on public sites by Church Personnel (whether official or personal) must reflect the values of our Catholic faith and should always follow the teaching of the Church. This includes, and is not limited to, posts, comments, photos, songs, videos, bulletins, blogs, and podcasts on both official Church websites and personal websites.

- Account settings for official sites should be set to maximize privacy.

- The site administrators are ultimately responsible for both the content they create and any other content appearing on the site.

- If you include a section on your official social media site for third-party comments, include a Code of Conduct for those comments. For example, the Code of Conduct on the USCCB's Facebook site is: "All posts and comments should be marked by Christian charity and respect for the truth. They should be on topic and presume the good will of other posters. Discussion should take place primarily from a faith perspective. No ads please." If possible, block anyone who does not abide by the Code of Conduct and delete inappropriate or offensive posts or comments. Whenever possible, pre-screen comments before they are posted and do not post inappropriate or offensive comments.

- Church social media sites should not include advertising for non-Church related websites, events, or products, except at the specific direction of the individual ultimately responsible for the site (for example, the pastor for parish sites). Comments that include solicitations or advertisements for non-Church related websites, events, or products should be deleted. Individuals that repeatedly include solicitations or advertisements for non-Church related websites, events, or products should be blocked, if possible.

- What you write is ultimately your responsibility. Participation in social media on behalf of the Archdiocese of Boston, its parishes, schools, and/or Archdiocesan Affiliated Organizations is not a right, but an opportunity, so please treat it with the utmost respect.

- Always remember that you represent the Church.

Compliance With Law and Church Policies

In establishing and managing social media sites, Church Personnel may not engage in any action that may violate federal or state law, the policies of the Archdiocese of Boston, any of its parishes or schools, any ministry or department of any parish or school, or any other Archdiocesan Affiliated Organization, or Canon Law. Copyright, trademark, trade secret, and other intellectual property laws prohibit the improper use of others' intellectual property. Do not post copyrighted materials, logos, trademarks, trade secrets, or similar materials without first obtaining the proper permission. If you ever have any question whether material may be protected by intellectual property laws, please contact a supervisor or the General Counsel of the Archdiocese of Boston **before** posting the material.

Church Personnel are prohibited from disclosing information that is understood to be held in confidence by the Archdiocese of Boston, any of its parishes or schools, any ministry or department of any parish or school, or any other Archdiocesan Affiliated Organization, including any information that is proprietary. This may include, for example, information about other employees including salaries and disciplinary records, information about ongoing crises and conflicts including ongoing litigation, information about students including educational records, and financial information about the Archdiocese, its parishes or schools or any Archdiocesan Affiliated Organization including lists of suppliers or vendors.

GUIDELINES:

- In order to protect both Church Personnel and users of official social media sites, all sites and postings must adhere to all policies of the Archdiocese, its parishes and schools, and any Archdiocesan Affiliated Organizations, including, without limitation, the Code of Ministerial Conduct, the Policies and Procedures for the Protection of Children, Archdiocesan Code of Conduct and Conflict of Interest Policy, the Electronic Use Policy, the Anti-Bullying Policy, the Anti-Harassment Policy, the Sexual Harassment Policy, HIPAA Guidelines, the Massachusetts Data Security Policy, and all other applicable published policies, procedures, and guidelines as may exist from time to time or as may be created or amended in the future.

- Logos or trademarks of the Archdiocese, its parishes and schools, or any Archdiocesan Affiliated Organizations may be used on personal websites only with the prior written approval of the applicable organization.

- In many cases, it is necessary to obtain the prior written consent of an individual to use such person's photograph or other likeness on a website. Should you have any questions in this regard, please contact the Office of the General Counsel of the Archdiocese.

- Appropriate photographs may be posted on official social media sites. Photographs of children should never be posted on social media sites without the prior approval of the child's parent or guardian ("parent") and under no circumstances should photographs of children with any identifying information be posted. If an individual requests that his or her photograph be removed (or, in the case of a minor, a parent makes such a request), that request should be promptly honored.

- Before using any images, video, music, or other documents, make sure you have looked for and understand the copyrights on that piece of work. The digital rights management issues of the music and film industries are particularly controversial and have led to a number of high-profile lawsuits and fines. It is best to avoid a potential legal problem by using only properly obtained and approved files.

- In addition, it is important to understand the rights of online written content. Just because you found something on Google does not make it free or available for use.

- When in doubt, seek permission from a supervisor or the General Counsel of the Archdiocese of Boston before posting.

Contact/Communication With Children

While social media can be a useful asset for the Church and its ministries, it can also be misused. Notwithstanding the informality of social media, it is most important to remember that in using social media, the boundary issues are the same as in person-to-person communication. Anyone using social media should be aware that children are highly likely to view and respond to materials posted online. Therefore, it is imperative that any Church Personnel posting online on behalf of the Archdiocese, its parishes and schools, or any Archdiocesan Affiliated Organizations be particularly careful in choosing what material to post and how to interact with children online. Most importantly, parents should constantly be made aware of any contact you may have with their children via social media.

GUIDELINES:
- Parents should be made aware of how social media is being used by the Archdiocese, its parishes and schools and any Archdiocesan Affiliated Organizations, be given an explanation of how to access such social media sites, and, to the extent possible, be

given the option to be emailed a copy of all material available to their children via such social media websites (including through the use of hyperlinks). While parents should be provided with the same material as their children, it does not have to be via the same technology (for example, if children receive a reminder via Facebook, parents can receive the same message via email).

- Make sure a minor's parent is always aware of any contact you may have with his/her child via social media. Parents can be informed either through written notice (for example, email) or personal contact (for example, face-to-face or over the phone).

- Ask parents, in writing, which forms of communication they prefer be used to contact their children. When communicating with minors electronically, obtain permission from parents to do so. If parents request their child not be contacted electronically, cease all electronic communication with the child.

- Do not request email addresses and phone numbers from children; this information should only be provided by parents. In the case of young children (i.e., elementary school and middle school students), only parents should be contacted directly.

- In the event minors are contacted directly by Church Personnel via email, parents must be copied on the content of all messages.

- Never post any information about a minor without the explicit permission of his/her parent.

- While the Archdiocese, its parishes and schools, and any Archdiocesan Affiliated Organizations are free to publicize their presence on social networking sites, minors should not be specifically sought out as "friends" (in other words, individually invited via site communication tools to associate with the group or page).

- Church Personnel should be encouraged to save copies of online conversations whenever possible, especially those that concern the personal sharing of a teen or young adult. If there is ever any doubt whether a conversation may be inappropriate, a supervisor should be contacted immediately, and the conversation should be terminated. If you receive an inappropriate personal communication from a minor, keep a copy of the message and inform your supervisor immediately.

- When communicating with a minor, write or speak as if you are also communicating with their parents. The boundaries that must be respected in oral communication extend to electronic communication. All communication must conform to Archdiocesan Policies and Procedures for the Protection of Children, the Code of Ministerial Conduct, and the Archdiocesan Code of Conduct and Conflict of Interest Policy. Communication that violates these policies will not be tolerated, regardless of the medium used to convey it, and may lead to discipline, up to and including termination.

Personal Websites

Church Personnel from time to time may create on their own initiative personal websites as a medium of self-expression. Church Personnel must recognize, however, that anything published on a personal website is no different from making such information available in any other public forum. Personal sites should reflect Catholic values. Any information that causes or has the potential to cause scandal or embarrassment to the Archdiocese, its parishes and schools, or any Archdiocesan Affiliated Organizations must be avoided.

If any Church Personnel choose to identify themselves as such on their personal website, many readers may assume they are speaking on behalf of the Archdiocese, its parishes and schools, or another Archdiocesan Affiliated Organization. In order to avoid any confusion, it is appropriate to include a brief disclaimer explaining that your website is personal and does not reflect the views of the Archdiocese, its parishes and schools, or any Archdiocesan Affiliated Organizations. For example, one may include:

"The views expressed on this website are mine alone and do not necessarily reflect the views of the Archdiocese of Boston or [NAME OF PARISH/SCHOOL/ARCHDIOCESAN RELATED ORGANIZATION]."

Even with this notice, any information that causes or has the potential to cause embarrassment to the Archdiocese, its parishes and schools, or any Archdiocesan Affiliated Organizations should be avoided and may, under certain circumstances, lead to discipline, up to and including termination.

GUIDELINES:

- Personal social networking sites should not be used for official ministerial purposes. Official sites of the Archdiocese, its parishes and schools, and any Archdiocesan Affiliated Organizations should not be used for personal purposes.

- Personal use of social media must be separate from business use.

- Logos or trademarks of the Archdiocese, its parishes and schools, and any Archdiocesan Affiliated Organizations may be used in an appropriate manner on personal websites only with prior written permission.

Monitoring and Discipline

The Archdiocese, its parishes and schools, and any Archdiocesan Affiliated Organizations should continually monitor all their official social media sites to ensure their consistency with Church teachings. The Archdiocese, its parishes and schools, and other Archdiocesan Affiliated Organizations may, under certain circumstances, have the right to review the personal websites of Church Personnel. Inappropriate posts, comments, photographs, songs, videos, bulletins, blogs, and podcasts on official sites may, under certain circumstances, subject the poster or the site administrator to discipline, up to and including termination.

GUIDELINES:

- Official social media sites must be frequently monitored for inappropriate posts. Inappropriate posts and comments should be promptly removed/deleted. A specific site administrator should be responsible for regularly monitoring such sites and removing inappropriate content.

- If third parties create unofficial groups or fan pages about the Archdiocese, its parishes and schools, and any Archdiocesan Affiliated Organizations, site administrators should, if legally permitted to do so, periodically review them for inappropriate content (for example, inappropriate use of logos, bullying, harassing, or defamatory language, etc.). You may report these pages/groups/users to the hosting site and ask that they be removed.

- Church Personnel should report to a supervisor any inappropriate use of organizational logos of the Archdiocese, its parishes and schools, and any Archdiocesan Affiliated Organizations.

- The Archdiocese, its parishes and schools, and any Archdiocesan Affiliated Organizations will not tolerate Church Personnel posting obscene, harassing, offensive, derogatory, defamatory, or otherwise potentially scandalous comments, links, and/or images which could discredit or cause embarrassment to the Archdiocese, its parishes and schools, or any Archdiocesan Affiliated Organizations, or any of their employees, volunteers, staff, vendors, partners, agencies, or schools. The posting of any such inappropriate material on official sites (or, under certain circumstances, on personal sites) may subject the individual posting such material to disciplinary action, up to and including termination.

- The Archdiocese of Boston reserves the right to make changes to these Guidelines at any time at its sole discretion. The Archdiocese, its parishes and schools, and any Archdiocesan Affiliated Organizations shall interpret and administer these Guidelines in light of changing circumstances and events.

- All Church Personnel who may create, monitor, add to, or otherwise utilize official social media sites of the Archdiocese, its parishes and schools, or any Archdiocesan Affiliated Organizations should sign an acknowledgment stating that they have received and read these Guidelines for the Use of Social Media.

ACKNOWLEDGMENTS

Immense gratitude. That is what I feel toward so many people who have helped me, a first-time author, take on this challenging project. Special thanks to:

- **Ximena and our three wonderful children, all gifts from God:** From the moment this book became a possibility, you supported the project enthusiastically. You put up with all the times I got up extra early in the morning to draft another chapter and needed to miss the evening and weekend activities to get this done. Thanks for your tremendous love and support!

- **Cardinal Seán O'Malley:** Your deep passion for evangelization and for using the media to reach people has guided all of my projects since you invited me to join the team at the Archdiocese of Boston in 2006. Thank you for supporting every one of our initiatives and ideas and encouraging our team to innovate!

- **Bert Ghezzi, George Foster, Greg Erlandson, Kyle Hamilton, Terry Poplava, Sharon Kaiser, and the great team from Our Sunday Visitor:** OSV has stayed true to its mission "to serve the Church," now into its second century. So much of what our new media team at the Archdiocese of Boston has accomplished was in partnership or friendship with the OSV Offertory division. I am honored that this book is being published by OSV! Thanks especially to Bert Ghezzi and George Foster for their wisdom, encouragement, and patience in editing this book.

- **My brother (Father) Roger; my parents, Roger and Midge; my brother Greg; my sister Colleen; and my entire family:** I have learned more about the Catholic faith from my brother Roger than any other source (read his homilies and articles at CatholicPreaching.com). My mom formed our hearts to think with the Church and love those in need. My father taught us how to go out of our way to serve others and instilled in us a work ethic that overcomes obstacles (which came in handy writing this book!). Colleen, you continue to inspire us. Greg, you show us how to be generous. Thank you for your unconditional love and support — from day one.

- **The great group at CatholicVoices USA,** who have a passion to communicate the Church through all forms of media. Thanks for your help in the book's final few months.

- **Andreas Widmer and Bob Allard:** Your wise and prayerful counsel has guided each major decision in my life over the past decade. Any man would be lucky to have great friends like you!

- **My former colleagues on the Archdiocese of Boston's new media and development teams:** Dom Bettinelli, George Martell, Karla Goncalves, Rick Heil, Anna Johnson, Damien DeVasto, Mary Jo Kriz, John Irwin and Patrick Gipson. It has been such a joy to be on a team with each of you daily and to work on so many initiatives together.

- **Our TGCL team:** The daily experience of participating in *The Good Catholic Life* radio program each afternoon has been the highlight of my professional life thus far. In addition to Dom, Rick, George, Karla, Stacia, and Anna, I honor our co-hosts Father Chris O'Connor, Father Matt Williams, Susan Abbott, Greg Tracy, Michael Lavigne, Father Roger Landry, Father Mark O'Connell and Father Chip Hines, our great guests, our sponsors Jim Wright and Chris Kelley, and everyone who invests an hour of their day to listen to the show.

- **Janet Benestad, Michael Lavigne, Bishop Arthur Kennedy, Father Paul Soper, Steve McDevitt, Beirne Lovely, and Terry Donilon:** This book, and the media efforts of the Archdiocese of Boston, would not have been possible without your help. Thanks for sharing the passion for *growing the Church through new media*!

- **The Pilot Media Group team**, led by Antonio Enrique. Your partnership allowed tremendous innovation in the archdiocese's Catholic media in the past few years. Each one of you has made a difference in my life: Christine Blanchette, Paul Blanchette, Marilyn Collins, Sean Gibney, Rose Lento, Michael McGrath, Stacia Morabito, Rick Mosley, Christopher Pineo, Larry Ricardo, Stephanie Rodricks, Michael Strong, Gregory Tracy, Nan Wilkins, and our Pilot New Media team (listed above). A special thanks to Frank Mendes and Dan Nisby, "adopted" members of our team.

- **Strong supporters of the archdiocese's Catholic media team**: Steve Barrett, Sister Marian Batho, Jan-Hein Cremers, John Corcoran, Thomas D'Arcangelo, John DeMatteo, Father Rich Erikson, Craig Gibson, Jay Gould, Jane Mancini Puliafico, John Monahan, John Riley, Jack Shaughnessy, Jo Tango, Tim Van-Damm, Scott Wahle, and Karl Wirth.

- **Pastors and priests in the Archdiocese of Boston,** particularly those who served with me on the Board of Trustees of The Catholic Foundation, those who have generously helped with TGCL, and to our wonderful parish priests at St. Agnes Parish, Father Brian Flatley and Father Jack Graham — thank you all for teaching me so much about leadership in the Church and for your inspirational and life-giving "Yes!" to God.

- **To every digital native and early adopter who has led the way in Catholic new media:** Thank you! I am particularly grateful to all of the parishes profiled in this book.

- **To everyone else who has helped in this project that I mistakenly forgot to mention:** Please forgive me!

NOTES

1. For a summary of Cardinal Seán's Holy Land trip, please visit http://www.cardinalseansblog.org/2013/04/12/ or www.TheGoodCatholicLife.com/holyland.

2. http://www.catholicpreaching.com/a-tremendous-comeback-and-victory-for-life-the-anchor-november-16-2012/.

3. A summary of our Rome coverage is at www.TheGoodCatholicLife.com/Rome. We completed 11 radio broadcasts, 23 blog posts on TheGoodCatholicLife.com, 1 episode of *Catholic Faith Essentials*, 15 photo albums (containing 600 photos), 3 *Pilot* articles, and 31 videos. We also brought several hundred prayer requests to the tomb of St. Peter.

4. "What it was like to be in St. Peter's Square the night Pope Francis was elected": http://www.thegoodcatholiclife.com/2013/03/14/what-it-was-like-to-be-in-st-peters-square-on-the-evening-of-3-13-13/ (accessed May 5, 2014).

5. Brandon Vogt, *The Church and New Media* (Huntington, IN: Our Sunday Visitor, 2011). Scot Landry contributed Chapter 7, "Innovative Shepherding: New Media in the Diocese."

6. Wikipedia definition of "New Media," http://en.wikipedia.org/wiki/New_media (accessed May 5, 2013): "New media refers to on-demand access to content any time, anywhere, on any digital device, as well as interactive user feedback and creative participation. Another aspect of new media is the real-time generation of new, unregulated content. Most technologies described as "new media" are digital, often having characteristics of being manipulated, networkable, dense, compressible, and interactive. Some examples may be the Internet, websites, computer multimedia, video games, CD-ROMs, and DVDs. New media does not include television programs (only analog broadcast), feature films, magazines, books, or paper-based publications — unless they contain technologies that enable digital interactivity. Wikipedia, an online encyclopedia, is an example, combining Internet accessible digital text, images, and video with web-links, creative participation of contributors, interactive feedback of users and formation of a participant community of editors and donors for the benefit of non-community readers. Facebook is an example of the social media model, in which most users are also participants."

7. Address of Pope Francis in a Meeting with the Bishops of Brazil, July 28, 2013 (accessed May 5, 2014), http://www.vatican.va/holy_father

/francesco/speeches/2013/july/documents/papa-francesco_20130727_
gmg-episcopato-brasile_en.html.

8. Message of the Holy Father Pope Benedict for the 43rd World Communications Day, "New Technologies, New Relationships. Promoting a
Culture of Respect, Dialogue and Friendship," released January 24, 2009,
for WCD on Sunday, May 24, 2009: http://www.vatican.va/holy_father
/benedict_xvi/messages/communications/documents/hf_
ben-xvi_mes_20090124_43rd-world-communications-day_en.html.

9. Matthew Kelly, *The Four Signs of a Dynamic Catholic* (Hebron, KY:
Beacon Publishing, 2012).

10. Sherry A. Weddell, *Forming Intentional Disciples: The Path to Knowing
and Following Jesus* (Huntington, IN: Our Sunday Visitor, 2012), p. 26.
Weddell analyzes the 2008 Pew Forum Religious Landscape Study on
Religious Affiliation.

11. Pope Francis, @Pontifex, October 27, 2013: https://twitter.com/pontifex.

12. Monsignor Paul Tighe, keynote address at 2013 Catholic New Media
Conference, October 19, 2013: http://www.pccs.va/index.php/en
/news2/attualita/item/1798-notes-from-msgr-paul-tighe-s-cnmc
-keynote-address?utm_source=twitterfeed&utm_medium=twitter.

13. Address of the Holy Father Francis to Participants in the Plenary Assembly of the Pontifical Council for Social Communications, September 21, 2013: http://www.vatican.va/holy_father/francesco
/speeches/2013/september/documents/papa-francesco_20130921_
plenaria-pccs_en.html.

14. Monsignor Paul Tighe, keynote address at 2013 Catholic New Media
Conference, October 19, 2013: http://www.pccs.va/index.php/en
/news2/attualita/item/1798-notes-from-msgr-paul-tighe-s-cnmc
-keynote-address?utm_source=twitterfeed&utm_medium=twitter.

15. Monsignor Paul Tighe, keynote address at 2013 Catholic New Media
Conference, October 19, 2013: http://www.pccs.va/index.php/en/
news2/attualita/item/1798-notes-from-msgr-paul-tighe-s-cnmc
-keynote-address?utm_source=twitterfeed&utm_medium=twitter.

16. Monsignor Paul Tighe, keynote address at 2013 Catholic New Media
Conference, October 19, 2013: http://www.pccs.va/index.php/en
/news2/attualita/item/1798-notes-from-msgr-paul-tighe-s-cnmc
-keynote-address?utm_source=twitterfeed&utm_medium=twitter.

17. Address of the Holy Father Francis to Participants in the Plenary Assembly of the Pontifical Council for Social Communications. Septem-

ber 21, 2013: http://www.vatican.va/holy_father/francesco /speeches/2013/september/documents/papa-francesco_20130921_ plenaria-pccs_en.html.

18. *Instrumentum Laboris* for the Synod for the New Evangelization, June 19, 2012: http://www.vatican.va/roman_curia/synod/documents /rc_synod_doc_20120619_instrumentum-xiii_en.html.

19. For more information on the technology adoption lifecycle, please visit http://en.wikipedia.org/wiki/Technology_adoption_lifecycle.

20. Robert Rivers, C.S.P., *From Maintenance to Mission: Evangelization and the Revitalization of the Parish* (Mahwah, NJ: Paulist Press, 2005).

21. Michael White and Tom Corcoran, *Rebuilt: Awakening the Faithful, Reaching the Lost, Making Church Matter* (Notre Dame, IN: Ave Maria Press, 2013), pp. xvi-xviii.

22. Ibid., pp. 277-278.

23. Pope Francis, @Pontifex, July 17, 2013: https://twitter.com/pontifex.

24. Code of Canon Law, 515 § 1: http://www.vatican.va/archive /ENG1104/__P1U.HTM.

25. *Catechism of the Catholic Church*, 2179, http://www.vatican.va/archive /ENG0015/_INDEX.HTM.

26. XIII Ordinary General Assembly of the Synod of Bishops, October 7-28, 2012, "The New Evangelization for the Transmission of the Christian Faith," Proposition 44: http://www.vatican.va/news_services /press/sinodo/documents/bollettino_25_xiii-ordinaria-2012/02_ inglese/b33_02.html.

27. Matthew Kelly: http://dynamiccatholic.com/mission/.

28. Pope Francis, @Pontifex, July 18, 2013: https://twitter.com/pontifex.

29. To learn more about the staff positions at Nativity Catholic Church in Brandon, Florida, please visit http://nativitycatholicchurch.org.

30. Message of Pope Francis for the 48th World Communications Day, "Communication at the Service of an Authentic Culture of Encounter," January 24, 2014: http://w2.vatican.va/content/francesco /en/messages/communications/documents/papa-francesco_20140124_ messaggio-comunicazioni-sociali.html.

31. Message of Pope Francis for the 48th World Communications Day, "Communication at the Service of an Authentic Culture of Encounter," January 24, 2014: http://w2.vatican.va/content/francesco

/en/messages/communications/documents/papa-francesco_20140124_messaggio-comunicazioni-sociali.html.

32. Vogt, *The Church and New Media* (Landry, Chapter 7), p. 117.

33. http://63.251.142.216/catholictvjr/default.aspx.

34. Various Catholic widgets, including daily Mass readings, can be found here: http://www.widgetbox.com/tag/catholic. Widgetbox has indicated that it will be ceasing operations in April 2014. Hopefully, another organization will aggregate good Catholic widgets. A simple Mass readings widget can be found here: http://www.catholiccontent.com/mass/.

35. http://www.stmonica.net and http://new.livestream.com/stmonica90403 (accessed on May 5, 2013).

36. http://catholictechtalk.com/2013/06/24/2013-parish-website-contest-winners/.

37. Cardinal Timothy Dolan, "God is everywhere, even on the blog!," October 9, 2009: http://cardinaldolan.org/index.php/hello-world/.

38. Scot Landry, "What it was like to be in St. Peter's Square when Pope Francis was elected": http://www.thegoodcatholiclife.com/2013/03/14/what-it-was-like-to-be-in-st-peters-square-on-the-evening-of-3-13-13/.

39. http://www.strangenotions.com/commenting/ (accessed on May 5, 2014).

40. Stanford University has many resources regarding the fair use of copyrighted material: http://fairuse.stanford.edu/overview/fair-use/what-is-fair-use/. Columbia University also has a good fair-use checklist: http://copyright.columbia.edu/copyright/files/2009/10/fairusechecklist.pdf.

41. http://www.google.com/analytics/.

42. Message of His Holiness Pope Benedict XVI for the 47th World Communications Day: http://www.vatican.va/holy_father/benedict_xvi/messages/communications/documents/hf_ben-xvi_mes_20130124_47th-world-communications-day_en.html.

43. http://michaelhyatt.com/a-social-media-framework.html.

44. http://whispersintheloggia.blogspot.com/2010/11/as-great-challenge-as-reformation.html.

45. The original link is inactive: http://en.wikipedia.org/wiki/Facebook_statistics. Updated link: http://en.wikipedia.org/wiki/Facebook (accessed on June 2, 2014).

46. The original link is inactive: https://newsroom.fb.com/Key-Facts. Updated link: https://newsroom.fb.com/company-info/ (accessed on June 2, 2014).

47. http://en.wikipedia.org/wiki/Facebook (accessed on May 5, 2014).

48. The original link is inactive: http://en.wikipedia.org/wiki/Facebook_statistics. Updated link: http://en.wikipedia.org/wiki/Facebook (accessed on June 2, 2014).

49. http://www.socialbakers.com/blog/1561-cutting-through-the-crowds-on-facebook-news-feeds (accessed on May 5, 2014).

50. http://expandedramblings.com/index.php/by-the-numbers-17-amazing-facebook-stats/ (accessed on May 5, 2014).

51. http://en.wikipedia.or/gwiki/Twitter (accessed on May 5, 2014).

52. Message of Pope Francis for the 48th World Communications Day, "Communication at the Service of an Authentic Culture of Encounter," January 24, 2014: http://w2.vatican.va/content/francesco/en/messages/communications/documents/papa-francesco_20140124_messaggio-comunicazioni-sociali.html.

53. 2013 Federal Reserve Payments Study, December 2013: http://www.frbservices.org/files/communications/pdf/research/2013_payments_study_summary.pdf.

54. http://www.catholic.com/blog/jimmy-akin/the-4-minute-speech-that-got-pope-francis-elected.

55. Book clubs may want to discuss Matthew Kelly's *Rediscover Catholicism* or *The Four Signs of a Dynamic Catholic*; Sherry Weddell's *Forming Intentional Disciples*; Father Michael White and Tom Corcoran's *Rebuilt*; Father Robert Rivers' *From Maintenance to Mission*; Austen Ivereigh's *How to Defend the Faith Without Raising Your Voice*; or Eugene Gan's *Infinite Bandwidth: Encountering Christ in the Media*.

56. http://dynamiccatholic.com/parish-book-program/.

57. *Catechism of the Catholic Church*: http://www.vatican.va/archive/ENG0015/_INDEX.HTM. *Compendium of the Catholic Church*: http://www.vatican.va/archive/compendium_ccc/documents/archive_2005_compendium-ccc_en.html.

58. http://www.usccb.org/issues-and-action/marriage-and-family/natural-family-planning/.

59. See www.PilotPrinting.net for parish or ministry rates.

60. All World Communication Day messages are linked here: http://www.pccs.it/gmcs/gmcs_eng.htm and http://www.fatherhardonmedia.org/wcd.html.

ABOUT THE AUTHOR

Scot Landry is the executive director of Catholic Voices USA, a lay media effort dedicated to increasing the number of well-catechized, media-ready Catholic communicators. Training offered by Catholic Voices seeks to form lay people to be media-friendly, studio-ready, ego-free, articulate speakers who explain Church teaching through letters to the editor, blog posts, op-eds, and radio and television interviews, as well as parish and other talks, with clarity and civility.

Prior to joining Catholic Voices USA in September 2013, Scot served as secretary for Catholic Media of the Roman Catholic Archdiocese of Boston, where he oversaw the archdiocese's media entities, including CatholicTV, *The Pilot* newspaper, Pilot Bulletins, Pilot Printing, Pilot New Media, and the Radio Apostolate. As a member of the steering committee of Cardinal Seán O'Malley's cabinet, he also was heavily involved in strategic planning, resource allocation, and implementation of major initiatives. He also hosted *The Good Catholic Life*, a live daily radio program on 1060AM WQOM in Boston. Scot had also served the Archdiocese of Boston as the cabinet secretary for Institutional Advancement for four years.

Prior to his service at the archdiocese, Scot was the chief operating officer at Eze Castle Software and Eze Castle Integration, a principal at The Parthenon Consulting Group, a Dean's Research Fellow at Harvard Business School, and a former brand manager at Procter & Gamble and James River Corporation.

Scot is the co-founder of the Boston Catholic Men's and Women's Conferences and won the 2008 "Ambassador of the Year" award from Legatus, a group for Catholic business leaders. He is a graduate of Harvard Business School and Harvard College.

Scot lives in suburban Boston with his wife, Ximena, and three children. He is proud that he was born and raised in Lowell, Massachusetts. His identical twin brother, Father Roger Landry, is a priest of the Diocese of Fall River.

Transforming Parish Communications: Growing the Church Through New Media is Scot's first book.

Blog: ScotLandry.com • **Twitter:** twitter.com/scotlandry
Website: ParishGuideToNewMedia.com